PALGRAVE POCKET

Palgrave Pocket Consultants are concise, authoritative guides that provide actionable solutions to specific, high-level business problems that would otherwise drive you or your company to employ a consultant. Written for aspiring middle-to-senior managers working across business at any scale, they offer solutions to the most cutting-edge issues across modern business. Be your own expert and have the advice you need at your fingertips.

Available now:

ATTRACTING AND RETAINING TALENT
Tim Baker

MYTH-BUSTING CHINA'S NUMBERS
Matthew Crabbe

RISKY BUSINESS IN CHINA
Jeremy Gordon

THE NEW CHINESE TRAVELER
Gary Bowerman

THE WORKPLACE COMMUNITY
Ian Gee and Matthew Hanwell

PEOPLE DATA
Tine Huus

MAKING SOCIAL TECHNOLOGIES WORK
Ronan Gruenbaum

CONVERSATIONS AT WORK
Tim Baker and Aubrey Warren

PUBLIC RELATIONS IN CHINA
David Wolf

Series ISBN 9781137396792

About the Author

A consultant, trainer and coach drawing on over twenty years' experience in public relations, advocacy, government communications, and social media, Charlie Pownall advises companies, governments and high profile individuals how to protect, manage and defend their reputations.

Previously Regional Managing Director (Asia-Pacific) at Burson-Marsteller, Group Communications Manager at WPP and a speechwriter and press officer at the European Commission, Charlie Pownall speaks regularly on reputation management, crisis communications and social media at business conferences, seminars, workshops, business schools, and universities. He also writes for *ClickZ*, *PR Week*, *Public Affairs Asia*, *Social Media Today* and other publications.

You can contact Charlie Pownall at **charliepownall.com**

Managing Online Reputation

How to Protect Your Company on Social Media

Charlie Pownall

First published 2015 by
PALGRAVE MACMILLAN

Palgrave Macmillan in the UK is an imprint of Macmillan Publishers Limited, registered in England, company number 785998, of Houndmills, Basingstoke, Hampshire RG21 6XS.

Palgrave Macmillan in the US is a division of St Martin's Press LLC, 175 Fifth Avenue, New York, NY 10010.

Palgrave Macmillan is the global academic imprint of the above companies and has companies and representatives throughout the world.

Palgrave® and Macmillan® are registered trademarks in the United States, the United Kingdom, Europe and other countries.

ISBN 978–1–137–38229–0

This book is printed on paper suitable for recycling and made from fully managed and sustained forest sources. Logging, pulping and manufacturing processes are expected to conform to the environmental regulations of the country of origin.

A catalogue record for this book is available from the British Library.

A catalog record for this book is available from the Library of Congress.

Typset by MPS Limited, Chennai, India.

Contents

List of Figures and Tables

Acknowledgments

It goes without saying that many people have had a hand in this book, and they all deserve my sincere thanks. First and foremost, to those who loaned me their time and expertise and helped me deepen my knowledge, marshal my thoughts, and review drafts: Ai-Leen Lim, Alex Johnston, Bronlea Mishler, Cayley Kochel, Chris Anderson, Christine Tran, Chris Wade, Cy Jervis, Ed Hoover, Eva Arevuo, Greg Mancusi-Ungaro, Isabelle Poirier, James Leavesley, James Murphy, James Turner, Joel Windels, Jonathan Wichmann, Joshua Steimle, Laura P. Thomas, Lauren Pell, Leslie Nuccio, The Hon. Mr Justice Warby, Miguel Bernas, Mimrah Mahmood, Michael Woodford OBE, Prashant Deorah, Ryan Holiday, Sam Flemming, Scott Peterson, Sourav Roy, Tatt Chen, Tom Liacas, Tom Linafelt, Vicky Kwong, William Beutler, Will Moss, Ximena Beltran Quan Kiu, Yuliya Yudina. Many thanks also to those who helped but did not wish to be named.

Tamsine O'Riordan, Stephen Partridge, Josephine Taylor, Isabel Jones and the team at Palgrave Macmillan patiently stuck with me, provided invaluable advice and feedback, and helped get this book off the ground. Without them it would not have been possible.

This book is not the product of one person's thinking and experience; rather it is the sum total of the collective wisdom, insights, and feedback provided by many colleagues, clients, and peers over the years. Particular thanks are due to colleagues past and present who provided me with strong mandates, collegial working environments, and a host of challenging clients and projects, among them Bill Rylance, Bob Elphick, Chris Robson, Feona McEwan, Geoff Martin, John Hunt, Matt Stafford, Sahala Sianipar, and Simon Pangrazio.

Preface

In May 2014 I received an invitation to help a national tourist board strengthen its online reputation. The stated objectives of the six-month program were to "Create honest, truthful and verifiable positive online reviews for _____[name redacted] tourism" and to "Push negative press past the second page in search engine results." Familiar stuff to anyone involved in the business of managing reputation on the web.

The back story, however, made the task less than straightforward. The country is an established tourist and business travel destination, but one whose receipts had nose-dived due to a major terrorist insurgency. International security experts were flagging the situation was worsening. Foreign governments warned travelers of a high threat of terrorism and kidnapping. Bombings and assassinations were regular events. And a single incident had forced the country and its detractors in dramatic and dreadful fashion onto the global news agenda.

The document went on to say the program should "Create barriers to any future negativity relating to the security issues and any other crises in _____ [name redacted]'" and that proposals should include details of "content creation (blogs, press releases, articles etc) and writing of engaging and relevant material to be uploaded to blogs, social media sites etc." In short, the tourism authority was looking to bury negative news and views on search engines and replace them with positive updates and wholesome praise in the midst of a severe national crisis. It also wanted to make it harder for negative opinion published online to gain visibility and traction. With so many people now using the internet to plan and buy their vacations, its concern was understandable. Yet its approach smacked of an institution with a limited understanding of how to protect and defend itself online.

* * *

There's little question that the folks at the tourist board faced a tricky challenge. Tasked with painting a positive picture of the country and rewarded (presumably) on the basis of the success of their efforts in persuading tourists and businesses to visit and operate there, they were instead confronted with a tidal wave of extremely disturbing and damaging stories, reviews, images, and videos being shared on TripAdvisor, YouTube, and elsewhere that all too graphically showed their country in chaos.

It is often said that the true test of a negative situation is how you handle it; the social web has the effect of making already difficult situations even more intimidating. Everyone seems to have an opinion about you, but few appreciate or understand the facts. Rumors and rants and misinformation abound. Thousands or even hundreds of thousands of people are taunting and ridiculing you on Twitter. Your Facebook page fills with ugly feedback and people haranguing each other. All of which makes it extremely tempting to turn inwards and pretend the problem is not happening. But behaving like an ostrich is not a realistic option in an environment that demands openness, honesty, and an instant response. And trying to dig your way out of trouble by burying the evidence on Google or Facebook, paying bloggers to say nice things about you, or organizing online mobs to undermine your enemies is guaranteed to make the hole deeper if you are discovered.

Why and how this book was written

I have spent the best part of 20 years helping companies, governments and individuals build, manage, and defend their brands and reputations, many of them focused online. Initially, much of my time was spent helping firms such as BP, Barclays, and WPP devise, develop, and manage corporate websites, intranets, and online communications and marketing programs. Yet while these channels and programs were seen as well designed and engaging and won awards, it was difficult to gauge their real value. To what extent were they actually changing the hearts and minds of the constituencies they were aimed at? In truth, we often had little idea.

Throughout this period I spent countless hours recording the ups and downs of companies, governments and governmental agencies, politicians, celebrities and sports people on the internet. Hundreds of examples litter my notebooks and, in recent years, my ever-handy Evernote account. Over the past decade, social media has come to dominate these jottings, and I found my focus shifting from brand building and management to instances of organizations being forced to defend themselves online. This focus was thrown into particularly sharp relief in June 2005 by the so-called "Dell Hell" saga, which saw the computer manufacturer mishandle journalist and pundit Jeff Jarvis after he had publicly taken it to task for shoddy products and poor customer service on his blog, leading to an acute and drawn out public relations disaster.[1]

Dell's meltdown was also notable as it was probably the first corporate collapse in social media to capture the attention of the mainstream media across the world, in part as it was seen to have contributed directly to significant drops in the computer manufacturer's customer satisfaction ratings and market share, and (perhaps coincidentally) share price. It also served to stimulate intense media interest in companies and individuals publicly self-destructing on the social web. At the time of writing this book, a Google search on the phrase "social media fail" returns over 200 million results.

Faced with a barrage of high profile meltdowns, and conscious of an increasing number of concerned clients, I found myself trying to find practical answers to three key questions:

1. How and why do corporate reputations come unstuck on the web and in social media?
2. What are the most effective ways of minimizing the risks of social media?
3. How should you respond to incidents and crises on the social web?

In addition to drawing on publicly available materials such as articles, commentary, and white papers, I reached out to organizations successfully managing and defending their online reputations to identify what they were doing well. Given that online reputation is a diffuse topic and covers many disciplines, some of which I am familiar with, others less so, I also talked to experts in fields such as defamation, privacy and intellectual property law, IT security, digital forensics, disaster emergency response, risk management, online activism, search engine marketing, and *Wikipedia* to dig deeper into specific areas and fill gaps in my knowledge and experience. This research became the foundation of a series of practical public and client workshops on online reputation management I have been running across Asia and the Middle-East over the last few years. It also forms the basis of this book.

How this book is structured

It is far from easy to manage and defend reputation in today's volatile, real-time environment. The team listening to online conversations can easily underestimate the implications of a seemingly innocuous online discussion. Traditional approval processes are slow and cumbersome. Lawyers take time to give a considered opinion. The social media team simply isn't qualified to answer difficult questions about their company's approach to climate change. By the time a response has been approved the story has gone global and journalists and bloggers are descending in droves to carve out the next angle.

Any half-decent communications or marketing professional will tell you that effective communication starts with understanding the audience. Yet this can be a real challenge when the expectations and behaviors of customers and stakeholders are evolving all the time and can be maddeningly unpredictable. Accordingly, we start (Chapter 1) by looking at the volatile nature of today's business environment and how customer and stakeholder expectations and behaviors are shifting online.

Part I considers how reputation is shaped by the social web and lays out the many different types of online threats (Chapter 2), before going on to explore the nature and impact of some of the more common threats, broken down into strategic and financial (Chapter 3); social and environmental (Chapter 4); behavioral and legal (Chapter 5); and operational and technological (Chapter 6) risks.

Thorough preparation may be nine-tenths of the law when it comes to the effective management of online reputation, but there will still be occasions when you are forced to defend yourself online publicly. **Part II** starts out by considering the broad range of options available when responding to online incidents (Chapter 7), before going to outline best practice principles and techniques for responding to a number of common scenarios playing out on the social web, including angry customers (Chapter 8), rogue employees (Chapter 9), activist attacks (Chapter 10), hostile journalists (Chapter 11), and backfiring marketing campaigns (Chapter 12).

Part III examines how crises are changing (Chapter 13), before going on to set out the nuts and bolts of a social media crisis plan (Chapter 14) – a crucial part of any organization's online armory – and the principles and practices that underpin how you can respond to (Chapter 15) and recover from (Chapter 16) a crisis using the internet and the social web.

What Managing Online Reputation is not

The social web presents an extraordinarily broad range of risks, each of which is more or less likely to occur depending on the organization, the context in which it is operating, and a host of other factors. *Managing Online Reputation* does not claim to cover all these threats, rather it tackles only some of the more common and most damaging of them. Nor does it set out to provide a template or silver bullet for each risk; every company and every action it takes presents its own set of vulnerabilities and opportunities, and a one-size-fits-all approach is simply not feasible or appropriate.

Who should read Managing Online Reputation

The social web impacts different industries and companies and the professionals responsible for managing reputation in different ways. In the days before Facebook and Twitter, proactive reputation defense was mostly the prerogative of oil firms, big pharma, tobacco and arms manufacturers, public sector, and other organizations in the public eye by dint of what they make or how they are seen to behave. More recently this list has been extended to include financial services firms and fast food. But with anyone now able to share their thoughts and experiences at any time, place and on whatever topic they choose, suddenly consumer goods companies, retailers, hotels, restaurants, e-commerce firms, legal and other professional services firms, indeed just about anyone and anything, big or small, global or local, find themselves more exposed than ever. While this book is largely written with commercial organizations in mind, it should also be useful to any entity doing business today.

Conscious of the damage that a poor reputation can wreak and the ease with which slip-ups can occur, reputation is increasingly viewed as a strategic imperative owned by the CEO and senior leadership. This book will give them something to chew on. But it also recognizes that the traditional model of corporate reputation managed by communications and corporate affairs professionals is effectively over and that marketing, sales, customer service, HR, legal, risk management, internal audit, and social media must all be actively involved and working more closely together. This book should be of value to professionals in any and all of these functions. Last but not least, *Managing Online Reputation* should also be of interest to business, communications, and marketing students, all of whom will have to deal in a professional capacity with the issues explored here over the course of their careers.

chapter 1

The New Abnormal

I write this book in an office with a birds-eye view of the Occupy protests in Hong Kong. Far below, a multi-colored tented village strewn with umbrellas, agitprop and Post-it Notes nestles uncomfortably between anonymous, glass skyscrapers. The days are eerily quiet. Steel and wooden barriers keep the traffic at bay while students at makeshift classrooms pore over accountancy manuals and medical histories, their movements tracked by the police, a phalanx of journalists, and gaggles of bemused tourists. It could be a scene lifted from a J.G. Ballard dystopia.

At night, the atmosphere transforms as locals stop by on the way home from work, and student leaders and politicians take to improvised platforms to call the government to account over its reluctance, unwillingness or inability to countenance more democratic elections. Suddenly a group of masked protestors moves close to the main stage and demands to speak, only to be turned away when they refuse to identify themselves. Angry, they start to dismantle one of the barricades but are turned back by outraged students. The mob, it transpires, has been organized in response to a post by a user called "Rather too naïve" on HKGolden, a popular local online community, that is calling for people to tear down the protestors' main speaking stage and replace it with one that anyone can use, not just the student groups and their acolytes.

Much of the ebb and flow of the protests is marshalled online. The two principal protest groups – Scholarism and the Hong Kong Federation of Students – use Twitter, Facebook, and Instagram to recruit and organize their troops and communicate their point of view. But the weapons of choice are Snapchat and FireChat. Snapchat is an encrypted mobile photo sharing service that enables users to set how long recipients can see their messages, while FireChat is a "mesh" mobile application that uses WiFi and Bluetooth links independent of internet connections or data networks, meaning messages can be delivered even if the internet is blocked or mobile networks are shut down. These kinds of tools enable people to communicate with groups of friends or sympathizers without having to worry about internet restrictions or, in the case of Snapchat, about being monitored or intercepted, meaning Hong Kong's student leaders can immediately and securely mobilize thousands of people at a moment's notice. Firechat was downloaded over 500,000 times in Hong Kong in the first 10 days of the protests.

Until recently, technologies of this nature would have been the preserve of governments and deep pocketed companies wanting to secure their communications. That they are now available to students is indicative of the degree to which the communications landscape has transformed. But this transformation is less about technology than about expectations and behavior, both of which are evident in five major shifts: the extraordinary speed with which information moves, widespread skepticism about big institutions and the media, the ease with which anyone can damage even the most reputable institution, the increasingly tribal and polarized nature of online communities, and the fickleness of opinion.

Information travels at warp speed

In November 2010, rumors of a crash of a Qantas A380 swept across the Internet. In fact, the plane's engine had only caught fire and it made a successful emergency landing in Singapore. Yet rumor became hard news as people shared eyewitness accounts online, especially on Twitter, which were quickly picked up by leading newswires and mainstream media outlets. Normally, the airline would have rushed to issue a holding statement to the media in order to buy it sufficient breathing space to get the actual facts. But in this case, the story had already gone viral, disseminated not by professional journalists but by ordinary people fascinated by the events and unbound by the need to check their facts and double-check their sources.

In 1710, Jonathan Swift quipped "Falsehood flies, and the truth comes limping after it." If only he were alive today. With every move and false move reported and scrutinized, it should come as little surprise that many organizations feel permanently under the gun and spend much of their time looking warily over their shoulders and scrabbling for a response. How fast information moves depends on many factors, from a firm's physical footprint to the strength of its reputation. Local online culture is also important. Online word-of-mouth in China, for example, travels at speeds that leave even the most experienced international executives slack-jawed, partly because of the sheer numbers of people involved, partly because much information in China is not commented upon, but cut and pasted immediately to weibo or WeChat, China's Twitter and WhatsApp equivalents.

Speed is also symptomatic of how exposed organizations are to online opinion. The more visible a company and the more widespread and entrenched its online detractors, the faster bad news about it circulates. When technology journalist Ryan Block called Comcast customer care to cancel his contract, his experience at the hands of one of its customer care representatives was so nightmarish he decided to record the experience half-way through the conversation. The recording, which he later posted online, shows the customer rep repeatedly demanding why Block was canceling the service and finding any way to stall him from doing so. The recording instantly went viral and has since been listened to almost 6 million times, covered extensively by the mainstream media and was even immortalized in a *New Yorker* cartoon. The fact that the discussion was recorded and could be accessed instantly by anyone certainly helped it go viral. But much of its visibility can be attributed to the fact that Comcast is widely disliked and has a reputation for lousy customer service, meaning it has to deal not just with an army of angry customers and bloggers regularly sounding off online, but also with an array of anti-Comcast online communities, websites, and blogs. News aggregator Reddit has a special section (aka "subreddit") with over 1,800 members "dedicated to venting about your shitty experiences with Comcast. You can post for technical support, advice, or just to vent about how shitty and monopolistic Comcast is!"[1]

Skepticism abounds

On July 23, 2011, lightening hit one of China's latest high-speed trains on a viaduct outside the south-eastern city of Wenzhou, causing it to collide with another train and killing 40 people and injuring nearly 200 others. The incident quickly caught the attention of the local and national media, which rushed to the scene only to discover eight mechanical diggers burying two of the carriages into freshly dug trenches. Their attempts were recorded on video and posted online, infuriating locals who promptly took to the Internet in droves to complain that the authorities were trying to cover up the accident. Subsequent attempts by Beijing to downplay the incident only made matters worse, with over 90% of people in an informal poll on Sina Weibo opting to describe the government's response as "terrible – it doesn't treat us as humans."

It is tempting for foreigners to believe Beijing reaps what it sows, but doubts about the degree to which governments and companies are acting in the best interests of their constituents are not limited to the Middle Kingdom. According to the Pew Research Center, trust in the US government dropped from 77% in 1964 to 24% in 2014.[2] Public relations firm Edelman's 2014 Trust Barometer revealed trust in government in many parts of the world had fallen to record low levels.[3] Business and the media also have their work cut out. Edelman's study also found that only a quarter of people say they trust CEOs to be honest and even fewer trust them to make decisions based on ethical and moral considerations.

This is not to say that skepticism or cynicism pervade every corner of the web; organizations with strong reputations are more than likely to be given the benefit of the doubt where a problem is seen as unusual and isolated. Yet those seen as behaving systematically poorly or inappropriately can expect to be lambasted online. Despite apologizing to Ryan Block and his girlfriend in person and via a statement posted to its website assuring that "The way in which our representative communicated with them is unacceptable and not consistent with how we train our customer service representatives," Comcast continued to receive an online lashing, a lashing that turned into a full thrashing once Block had uncovered a thread on Reddit posted by a former Comcast employee stating that the firm employed dedicated "Retention Specialists" compensated by the number of customers they manage to keep on board.

Even the most highly regarded firms can be ridiculed mercilessly if they are seen to be deliberately misleading their audiences. In 2012, General Mills was named the "Most Reputable Company in

America" by the Reputation Institute. But when the cereal maker updated its legal terms two years later so that its customers could no longer sue the firm, and tried to do so under the radar by merely updating the relevant pages on its website, a public outcry ensued. It reversed course two days later. But by claiming its terms – and the company's intentions – had been "widely misread,"[4] even its reverse caused significant friction.

The mainstream media fares little better. Until recently, reputable newspapers such as *The New York Times*, *The Times of India*, and *Yomiuri Shimbun* (Japan and the world's biggest selling newspaper with over 10 million daily readers) or broadcasters like the BBC played a vital role in determining what people read about and, by extension, what they did not read about. But with classifieds disappearing to free listing sites like Craigslist and with news commoditized, publishers are under huge pressure to publish faster, cut costs and be more opinionated. And this has led to a rash of fictitious, inaccurate and skewed articles, giving readers additional reasons to migrate to the likes of *Business Insider*, *Buzzfeed*, and *Vox*. This migration may prove permanent: *Business Insider* now boasts more readers than *The Wall Street Journal*.[5]

Worryingly, these new players can bring very different editorial standards, mixing hard news and "native advertising" (branded company content dressed up as semi-independent feature stories), analysis and publisher-owned consultancy services, animated gifs and kitten photos in a manner reminiscent of the bawdy Yellow and Penny Presses of the eighteenth and nineteenth centuries. As Ryan Holiday sets out in his coruscating book *Trust Me, I'm Lying* (for a precis, see Twelve Useful Books on Online Reputation at the end of this book), the fact that bloggers working for *Buzzfeed* and other tabloid-esque outlets are paid by the number of page views their stories generate means facts are routinely ignored in the race to break a story or secure a new angle. And once *Buzzfeed* runs a story, it is far more likely that it is going to be picked up by CNN or the *Daily Mail Online*. The end result is a vicious circle in which half-truths, partial truths, and outright falsities are peddled by all levels of the media and are consumed by a public disinterested in the facts and willing to believe the worst. No wonder people are skeptical.

Anyone can wield a lightsaber

If you have seen *Star Wars* you will remember the lightsaber, the sword-like weapon used in close combat by the Jedi Knights and the Sith. Made from plasma and suspended in a force containment field lightsabers were heavy and awkward to use, but a weapon to be feared in the hands of an expert. "Anyone can use a blaster or fusioncutter," noted Obi-Wan Kenobi in *Star Wars Episode IV*, "but to use a lightsaber well was a mark of someone a cut above the ordinary." A few months ago, having received a check for some work I had completed in Singapore, I went to my local HSBC Business Bank branch in Hong Kong expecting to deposit the funds quickly and easily, only to be told the transaction would be subject to an unexpectedly large charge and take three weeks to clear. Surprised and irritated, I took to Twitter to express my displeasure. To its credit, the bank publicly responded in a couple of hours, even if it was just to suggest I contact its UK call center. Clocking into my Internet banking account a few days later, I was pleasantly surprised to find that the check had already cleared and the charges had been reduced. With Twitter at my disposal, I figure I have a much better chance of making my case if I use a blaster to escalate a complaint than if I take the conventional route of filling out a form and hoping for the best, or even writing to my bank manager.

When Hasan Syed's parents lost their luggage traveling from Chicago to Paris in August 2013, he unsheathed a lightsaber. Fed up with the way British Airways was handling the issue, Mr Syed took to Twitter. But instead of simply tweeting his complaint, he bought USD 1,000 of "promoted tweets" via Twitter's self-service ad-buying platform to warn people that the airline's customer service was "horrendous" and that they "can't keep track of your baggage." And he threatened to keep running the ads until BA found his parents' belongings.

Compared to traditional advertising, promoted tweets are cheap, highly focused (they can be targeted geographically, by language, gender, interest and a host of other options.), and can be tracked and improved in real-time. In this case, Syed aimed his ad at followers of BA's Twitter profiles in the US and UK. But this being the first time an individual had bought advertising on Twitter to attack a big, global company, it also attracted the interest of the media. Within six hours, the high-profile US-based technology blog *Mashable* had picked up and run his story, resulting in a wave of re-tweets, blog posts, and media coverage from the BBC, *Mail Online*, *Huffington Post*, *NBC News* and hundreds of other news outlets and blogs around the world.

Of course, Hasan Syed is far from alone in recognizing the power of social media; nowadays anyone with Internet access can take to Twitter or Facebook to get something off their chest. For example, employees now have a powerful weapon to use against their employers (a fact not lost on US government whistleblower Edward Snowden). It is also far easier for businesses or jilted lovers to spread rumors about their competitors – all that is needed is a fake name and an email address unconnected with the company.

The geographical playing-field has also been flattened. A blogger in one country can now say something completely untrue about an individual or company and be reasonably confident that he is not going to get dragged into a legal dispute thanks to the inconsistency of legal regimes. Data hacks are routinely orchestrated from other countries, as Sony Pictures discovered in late 2014, when it suffered a huge leak of internal emails, documents, and personal details of employees that was purportedly planned and executed in North Korea.

The ability to damage a firm, then, is no longer limited to those with the right connections. Threats can now be made by just about anyone, at any time, from any place and in ways that are expressly designed to cause maximum disruption and reputational damage.

Tribalism fuels animosity

One of my earlier experiences building and managing online communities was to help a group of business people, economists, and politicians devise and run a website on Europe's single currency. It was the late 1990s, against a background of high fever in the UK about the prospect of European monetary union and whether or not Britain would join, and the idea was to provide useful, factual information for British businesses faced with having to deal with a massive trading block operating in a powerful new and foreign currency on its doorstop, and a neutral place where they could discuss the latest issues and ask for advice.

Unsurprisingly the task of keeping the community focused on the matter at hand – the practicalities of the single currency for British business, as opposed to the vexed political question of Britain's role – proved challenging. Most users of the site visited to gain a better understanding of the issues and, even if they were anti-single currency or flat out anti-European, they appreciated its neutral stance and stuck to its clearly stated rules of engagement. Yet a small and vocal minority persistently tried to disrupt matters and turn the community into an extension of the brawling going on in Parliament. On a couple of occasions it was hacked.

Fortunately, the vocal minority never got to dominate the majority, partly as we rigorously ensured that the content published and the discussions taking place on the site did not overstep the mark. People who did were warned and if they transgressed again were banned. But managing online communities and discussions in those days was relatively straightforward. Fewer people were online, and they were less sophisticated in how they used technology to make their point. More pertinently, there was no Facebook or LinkedIn or YouTube to speak of, meaning that there were far fewer places for people to congregate and talk about their interests, and the sites that did exist were relatively difficult to use and provided no way for people to follow one another as individuals or as groups. Backlashes were largely confined to the community where discussions were taking place or to email campaigns.

Fast-forward a decade or so and I was leading the team managing a number of Facebook pages and Twitter profiles for a large Chinese manufacturer of telecoms equipment and smartphones. A young company, it had catapulted itself into the global premier league in both categories by providing high quality products at low cost and, being a private firm, it was able to use the proceeds to invest in R&D and its people, rather than give it back to investors. It is in many ways a remarkable story; but it is also one clouded in controversy. Huawei – the firm in question – was seen to be too close to the Chinese military and government, to have benefitted unfairly from state aid, and to have copied competitors' technologies. There was also the fact that a number of governments around the world, notably Washington, were concerned its technologies could be used for surveillance and constituted a national security threat.

Working on the account provided an unusually close-up view of how different types of customers and stakeholders with different backgrounds, beliefs, views, and experiences intersect online. On the one hand, there were plenty of people who were genuinely impressed by its products and the value they represented. Some may not have known the firm was Chinese, but most did and were perfectly willing to give it the benefit of the doubt. On the other hand, a reasonable proportion had bought its products, reckoned them to be sub-par and felt its customer support was not so much poor as non-existent. There were also numerous other sub-groups, from those who detested the fact that the firm was Chinese to those worried about its environmental credentials. There was also a sizable number of people anxious to get a job at a fast-rising firm reckoned to treat its people better than many of its Chinese counterparts.

With so many conflicting interests, an unhealthy proportion of the interaction was ugly. Even if many people lamented the quality of Huawei's customer care, discussions were frequently interspersed with people accusing it of anything and everything, from spying on the Indian government to supporting the Taliban and propping up broke African governments. People who openly praised Huawei were regularly singled out as lackeys or traitors. At one point, around 7,000 Venezuelans took to the firm's global Facebook page to accuse it of lying about a commitment it had made to provide upgrades to some of its phones, an attack that was clearly timed to coincide with the biggest mobile industry event of the year in Barcelona.

Huawei elicits unusually strong opinions, but the Internet has also become a significantly more brittle, polarized environment since the advent of social media. Much of this has to do with the fact that you have to opt-in and select who and what you want to listen to, resulting in an entrenched sense of tribalism from the get-go. And in this environment, online opinion is driven as much by emotion as by facts. Say something controversial or that goes against the grain of the community and the backlash is immediate and unforgiving.

The fickleness of opinion

In 2000, around the time the mobile revolution took root, the average human attention span was reckoned to last around 12 seconds. Research shows we are now only able to concentrate for 8 seconds; one second less than a goldfish. As our attention spans have dwindled, so apparently has our capacity to think through matters logically and deeply; leading our expectations and behaviors to chop and change like ships without a sail. In turn life has become all the more challenging for companies. Take the infamous hack of Sony Pictures late 2014. Initial reaction to the breach was mostly limited to speculation about who might have caused it and that it may have been connected to the movie house's upcoming release of *The Interview*, a comedy depicting the assassination of North Korea leader Kim Jong Un. But then the salaries and social security numbers of over 47,000 current and former Sony executives, freelancers, and film stars were leaked, quickly followed by details of the firm's security certificates, server access keys, and passwords for just about every aspect of its IT system and its many social media accounts, the details of the aliases used to conceal the identities of celebrities, and the email inboxes of senior Sony staff, including its CEO, and marketing plans. Big and legitimate questions started to be asked about the quality of Sony's information security. But the narrative quickly shifted again, as elements of the media homed in on emails appearing to show bigotry, racism, sexism, and harassment at the firm.

Suffice to say we eagerly lapped up the latest and most obnoxious email and the steady drip of celebrity gossip – a squirming Sony was much the best entertainment to come out of Hollywood for years. Yet the episode also raised important issues about privacy and the public interest, questions that reverberated across many parts of the media as well as the broader general public. Is the media acting as little more than Pyongyang's attack dog? Should all information in the public domain be considered "neutral" and therefore free to be analyzed, publicized, and manipulated at will? Or should caution be exercised to protect confidential information and people's privacy? What exactly is the public's interest in this instance?

To be sure, Sony's hack was unusual: the scale of the breach was unprecedented, it involved celebrities, top Hollywood executives and even British royalty, and appears to have been perpetrated by one of the US' most fervent enemies. But the incident points to a broader truth: that for all the tribalism and partisanship, few of us have the time or even the inclination to take a firm and considered stance on many things. So either we stick to what we already know or we go with the wind.

The fickleness of online opinion presents organizations with great opportunities and challenges. People are open to persuasion on many issues, even if it requires a close understanding of their personal prejudices and requirements. But with trust in many companies and brands low, and false, misleading, and deliberately provocative information constantly swirling, people can turn on you and your brand at a moment's notice and for no clear reason.

* * *

Expecting the unexpected is essential in a world in which the abnormal has become everyday. But with so much noise, which signals are relevant and which need to be taken seriously? What and who can be trusted? In *The Art of War* Sun Tzu argued that, "If you know your enemy and know yourself, you need not fear the result of a hundred battles." Understanding the expectations and behaviors of one's detractors is essential in today's environment, as is having an objective understanding of one's own weaknesses. But first it is necessary to have some kind of framework for thinking about the threats posed by the social web and how these impact existing threats to your business and reputation.

part I

Understanding the
Threats

chapter 2

Defining Online Reputation Threats

On November 22, 2011, Qantas took to Twitter to ask:

> "Ever wanted to experience Qantas First Class luxury? You could win a First Class gift pack feat. a luxury amenity kit and our famous QF PJs."
>
> "To enter tell us What is your dream luxury inflight experience? (Be creative!) Answer must include #QantasLuxury."

Within an hour the campaign was trending on the micro-blog platform, but not for the reason the airline had been hoping. Instead, responses lampooned the campaign and Qantas' product and customer service.

> For @Ivalaine "#qantasluxury having a skybed so 'superior in its class' you have to be under 5 foot to be able to use it with your legs straight."
>
> Another quipped "#QantasLuxury? 1. Plane takes off/ arrives on time; 2. Baggage delivered promptly. This used to be called #QantasService."
>
> For another customer "Qantas Luxury is getting my flight refund back after waiting almost a month."

A host of earlier and ongoing issues impacting the company were also highlighted, including persistent questions surrounding the safety of the airline's planes in the wake of the A380 that had caught fire outside Singapore a year earlier and the failure of an engine in early November 2011 that had led to a flight carrying comedian Stephen Fry to London diverting to Dubai. The campaign was also run against a background of significant industrial unrest sparked by a controversial plan announced by Qantas management in August 2011 to restructure the airline's international division and to cut an estimated 1,000 jobs in its domestic market, eventually leading to the last-minute grounding of the airline's entire fleet in late October. To compound matters, CEO Alan Joyce had just been awarded a pay increase of 71%.

> One Tweeter reckoned the phrase meant "#QantasLuxury is a massive executive bonus while your workers starve and your former customers choke."
>
> For another "Qantas Luxury means sipping champagne on your corporate jet while grounding the entire airline, country, customers & staff."
>
> Another Twitter user prayed for "Flights that leave on schedule because Management doesn't arbitrarily shut down the airline #QantasLuxury."

To its credit, Qantas realized quickly that its promotion was going astray and, deploying a dose of deadpan Aussie humor ("At this rate our #QantasLuxury competition is going to take years to judge"), attempted to curtail the worst of the fall-out. But the real damage was yet to come in the form of a tsunami of humiliating mainstream, business, and trade media headlines across the world.

How the social web impacts reputation

There was nothing intrinsically wrong with Qantas' Luxury campaign. It was creative and found a way of getting people to sit up,
take notice, and start talking. But the airline got two key things
wrong: the campaign was poorly timed and it failed to take into
account the wider public mood, thereby inadvertently providing a
platform for people to vent their frustration and anger about the
company. The result was massive negative publicity and a tailwind
of damaging digital detritus.

The episode demonstrates the three ways the social web shapes
reputation (Figure 2.1):

Ignites. Occasionally someone in your company is going to do or
say something online – mouth off against a competitor, fail to
take care of an important blogger, or run a campaign that is seen
as silly, unprofessional, inappropriate, or unethical – that triggers
people to express their displeasure or ridicule you. #QantasLuxury
fits into this bracket. There are also times when your social media
defenses may be breached or you may be deliberately provoked

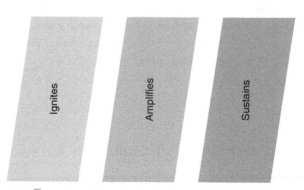

FIGURE 2.1 Role of social media in shaping reputation

Source: Charlie Pownall.

by an activist, competitor, former employee, or troll, resulting in a wave of negative feedback and media coverage.

Amplifies. Abraham Lincoln famously quipped that "Character is like a tree and reputation like a shadow. The shadow is what we think of it, the tree is the real thing." Think of the social web as your shadow, reflecting and amplifying what people think and feel about you. Amplification works in two ways: a company with a reputation for innovation and great products will be lauded online, whereas a firm with poor customer service or other failings will be routinely castigated. Qantas' Twitter campaign may have made the airline look naïve and somewhat stupid but the real damage was done by people venting about poor customer service and expressing their frustration and anger about its industrial dispute and the double standards it was seen to involve.

Sustains. Unlike real-world conversations, which are limited by time and place, discussions in social media ebb and flow and expand and contract as people enter and leave the fray. And the more animated or controversial the discussions the more likely they are to be referenced by bloggers and the media and indexed and shown in search engine results, meaning they can be sustained for weeks, months, or even longer.

Four years after it went astray, #QantasLuxury continues to be talked about online and the hashtag is still used to bash the airline, reinforcing broader perceptions that the airline has been foundering. By mid-2012 Qantas' reputation had slumped from 8th in 2011 to 25th in an annual ranking of Australia's top corporate brands[1] and it had lost its long-established lead in domestic customer satisfaction to Virgin Australia.[2]

Real amplification still requires the mainstream media

Reputational issues may be triggered, amplified, and sustained online but it is a mistake to believe they are somehow separate from other media. Twitter may have triggered an outpouring of complaints about Qantas yet the incident only went truly viral when the likes of the *Sydney Morning Herald*, the BBC, and CNN got involved. The fact is, despite massive fragmentation of audiences and channels, the emergence of Facebook, Reddit and other platforms, the disappearance of classifieds to Craigslist, and all manner of other challenges, the mainstream media lives on and remains the most credible and influential source of information and news for most people.

The staying power of the mainstream media is evident in the process by which many news stories break. Vividly described by Ryan Holiday, it starts with cash-strapped, page view-hungry bloggers constantly scouring Twitter, Facebook comments, consumer review sites, bulletin boards, corporate websites, and SEC filings for stuff to write about. Bloggers may mostly be writing about personal stuff or their local community but they are always on the lookout for big stories to attract new readers. If a story is sufficiently well researched, juicy or unusual it stands a good chance of being picked up by an online journalist, most of whom use bloggers as sources and filters for their own output and whose editorial standards are usually lower than those of the legacy print or broadcast media. And a strong story run on *Forbes* or *The Huffington Post* will be widely shared on Facebook and Twitter, meaning that it is much more likely to get picked up by CNN or the BBC. And when these outfits run the story so does everyone else.

Defining social media risks

The social web is a crucial prism through which every aspect of your organization is endlessly passed and refracted, providing huge opportunities if you have great products, funky offices that people would die to work in, and a charismatic, open-necked leader, and significant challenges if you are hide-bound by strict hierarchies, slow decision-making, and me-too products.

However social is not just about reputation. It is about how you support your customers, recruit your people, and transfer skills and knowledge across the many different parts of your business. As such social media poses many different kinds of business challenges and risks, from the power of customers to hold you to account, to a host of strategic, operational, and legal issues.

Nonetheless damage to reputation is frequently seen as the single biggest threat posed by the social web, followed by the disclosure of personal data and the release of confidential information. Digital research and consulting firm Altimeter Group identifies the most serious business risks of social media as shown in Figure 2.2.[4] Yet in reality every threat listed by Altimeter constitutes a threat to one's reputation to a greater or lesser extent. For instance, untrue or defamatory statements about your leadership or employees constitute a direct threat to your reputation, while so-called "social engineering attacks" (or attacks on your technology infrastructure through your social media presence) can cause huge damage to your business though, given their regularity, often have a relatively minor reputational impact.

What then are the threats of social media and what impact do they have on reputation? A useful way to approach this question is to categorize the risks using conventional risk management groupings (Figure 2.3):

- **Strategic**. Issues that may impact the performance and reputation of the business as a whole, including marketplace changes, lack of innovation, and political change or intervention.

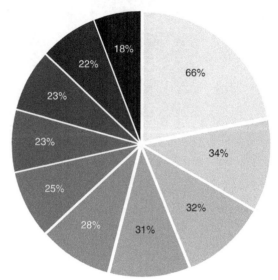

FIGURE 2.2 Critical or significant risks to business from social media
Source: Altimeter Group, 2012.

- **Financial**. The possibility of an organization and/or its shareholders losing money through lost revenue, increased capital costs, or destruction of shareholder value.
- **Societal**. Social, cultural and environmental issues that may negatively impact an organization, such as nationalism or a failure to meet evolving expectations about pollution, health, obesity, or food safety.
- **Behavioral**. Risks resulting from illegal or unethical behavior by an organization's employees or partners, including bribery, money laundering, sexual misconduct, and equal opportunities.

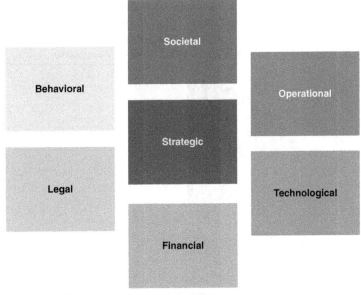

FIGURE 2.3 / **Categories of risks to reputation**

Source: Charlie Pownall.

- **Legal**. Threats to an organization's reputation arising from the loss of intellectual property, lack of compliance, changes in the law, litigation, and other factors.
- **Operational**. Threats from unauthorized or incorrect actions and from breakdowns in day-to-day processes, including production, customer experience, supply chain management, and employee health and safety.
- **Technological**. IT system disruptions and the malicious or accidental theft, disclosure, or destruction of company and customer information and data.

✱ ✱ ✱

Starting with strategic and financial risks, over the next four chapters we'll explore some of the top vulnerabilities associated with social media and examine how these can impact your reputation.

3

Strategic and Financial Threats

The Dawn of Glad Tidings is an app with a difference. Freely available on the web and Google Play, "Dawn" keeps its users up-to-date on the latest news from IS (Islamic State). It also automatically posts content in their names, peppering volleys of tweets, hashtags, and images to their followers and beyond, each volley programmed to be posted sufficiently far enough apart to avoid Twitter's spam detection software. Dawn's users are IS' propaganda foot soldiers, helping their master get its message out online and the group's advances are accompanied by waves of thousands of tweets showing jihadists brandishing the group's black flag.

Dawn is only one small element of a much broader and highly sophisticated effort that sees IS fighters tweeting live from the battlefield, answering questions from potential recruits on music sharing sites, getting thousands of their supporters to tweet and retweet barrages of messages at specific times of the day so that they trend on Twitter, developing video games simulating terror attacks, sharing battle summaries on information sharing sites such as JustPaste, and, most infamously, publicizing the executions and beheadings of prisoners. A 2014 study by the Brookings Institution identified between 46,000 and 70,000 accounts on Twitter supporting the movement.[1] IS even has its own media production units that co-ordinate the group's propaganda activities, churning out photos, graphics, videos, documentaries, English language magazines, and even annual reports.

The Islamic State sees the social web as an opportunity to galvanize support amongst young people, drive recruitment, and to paint a picture of itself as an organization that knows exactly what it is doing and that is remorselessly gaining ground on its opponents. It also uses Twitter and other social platforms to paint a picture of normal civic life, showing women going about their daily lives, tending children and cooking, seemingly unaffected by the horrors of war. In all, its efforts enable it to exert "an outsized impact on the how the world sees it," according to the authors of the Brookings study.

In business terms IS' use of social media is akin to an unexpected and extremely aggressive marketplace assault that leaves its competitors – primarily Arab governments but also rival Islamic groups – with little option other than to fundamentally re-appraise how they can compete. Yet, still raw from the Arab Spring uprisings in 2010, 2011, and 2012, many Middle-eastern governments continue to view social media as a threat to social stability, routinely block the internet, censor online content, and continue to use stodgy government-owned news agencies and compliant traditional media outlets to get their message across.

Of course, Arab governments are hardly in a minority – their counterparts across the world find themselves having to think long and hard about what social media means for them. Likewise companies. Research by Deloitte/*Forbes Insights* shows that corporate leaders think the risks of social media rank alongside financial risk as one of the single largest threats to their businesses.[2] But what are the strategic risks of social media and how do they impact reputation? Major changes to the dynamics of a marketplace such as those meted out by IS constitute one type of threat, as do substantial shifts in customer and stakeholder opinions and behavior. Others include lack of innovation and geopolitical and socio-economic shifts, all of which can have a direct impact on an organization's strategic and financial performance.

Strategic and financial threats tend to have an indirect impact on reputation. Companies underestimating the nature and pace of change can be seen as slow, unimaginative, and risk averse, and can quickly lose the confidence of their customers, employees, and other audiences. The poverty of the response by some governments to the newfound power their citizens wield raises serious questions about their competence, credibility, accountability, and in some cases their legitimacy. Strategic and financial threats that can also impact reputation more directly. Rumors fly through the digital ecosystem calling into question the quality of your management, the wisdom of your strategy, or the benefits of your products. Social media has also made it much easier for competitors and other vested interests to attack your reputation, either directly or covertly.

Inadequate board oversight

Social media is often considered a grassroots phenomenon that disrupts the existing order. In their book *Groundswell*, Charlene Li and Josh Bernioff described the effect of social technologies as, "A social trend in which people use technologies to get the things they need from each other, rather than from traditional institutions like corporations."[3] The pressures may be bottom-up but much hinges on how company leaders respond in terms of developing an appropriate strategic framework for their organization, managing the risks, and strengthening internal and external defenses.

The CEO and board of directors are ultimately responsible for managing and protecting an organization's good name. And with social media now playing an important role in almost every organization's future, it is essential that those at its apex are aware and on top of the risks. This can be challenging: board members and senior leaders are much less likely to use Facebook or have a detailed understanding of how social media impacts reputation. Yet the CEO and board are ultimately accountable for the strategy of the company and for ensuring that the risks to the business as a whole and its reputation are effectively managed.

Strategy and planning

Social technologies are now widely adopted at many institutions. Having started out with marketing and public relations, both areas that continue to undergo profound changes as a result of listening to and participating in online conversations, many institutions have been expanding their use of social media to sales and customer service. And now the focus is on integrating social across the entire breadth and depth of their organizations, from human resources, recruitment, and internal communications to product development and business planning.

Initially it was difficult to quantify the benefits of using social media, yet companies now report they are seeing significant improvements in their ability to win new customers and deepen customer loyalty. According to research by McKinsey, the more broadly and deeply firms adopt social technologies the bigger the reported benefits,[4] notably through increasing speed to access knowledge and reducing communications and travel costs. The opportunities are huge. McKinsey estimate that some USD 900 billion to 1.3 trillion can be unlocked through improved communication and collaboration within and across companies within the consumer goods, financial services, professional services, and advanced manufacturing industries alone.[5]

However getting from A to B can be a fraught process. Organizations that are slow, hierarchical, siloed, and risk-averse struggle with the openness and speed of decision-making that the social web demands.

A lack of clarity about compliance has held up firms in healthcare, financial services, and other regulated industries. There also remains a paucity of talent, and many companies still find themselves unable to quantify the benefits of the social web. Furthermore change can be difficult when senior leaders are not digital or social natives.

Unsurprisingly strategic mistakes continue to be made that can lead to lower market share, increased costs, lower margins, and lower customer and employee satisfaction. Often these take the form of a failure to see major changes in the marketplace driven by quick-thinking competitors and new entrants, or by the fast-changing expectations and behaviors of customers and other stakeholders, and to change and innovate accordingly; insufficient integration of the social web across the organization, most evident in treating social media as a silo that fails to co-operate or be taken seriously by others; inadequate governance, including the lack of a board-level champion, inadequate or poorly understood policies and protocols such as those governing the behavior of employees online; or insufficient budget and inadequate means to capture and measure the value of one's social media activities.

Risk and reputation management

Another major risk is a failure to understand the risks and manage the reputational aspects of social media effectively. In large part this is attributable to a failure amongst companies to understand what people really think about and want from them, either offline or online or both. Qantas' Luxury campaign spiraled out of control principally as the airline had failed to take into account the breadth and depth of anger Australians felt towards it over its restructuring and its underwhelming service. Another reason why many organizations have downplayed the reputational aspects of the social web is the tendency to approach the medium primarily as a tool to increase awareness and build online buzz and sales through product campaigns and promotions rather than as a long-term business, brand-building and reputation management tool, also epitomized by the #QantasLuxury debacle.

At a time when reputation risk is seen as increasingly important, this can seem strange. Doubtless conscious of the damage suffered by financial firms during the recent financial crisis and of meltdowns of the kind experienced by Tesco after it had overstated its accounts or resulting from allegations of widespread corruption at Walmart Mexico, research studies consistently show reputation risk as one of the top, if not the top, risk facing companies today. For example, a 2014 study of 320 board members of USD 500m+ companies across the world by law firm Clifford Chance and the Economist Intelligence Unit found that reputation risk is now regarded as the second most important risk after financial risk.[6] A 2014 Deloitte survey of senior global executives discovered that 87% of respondents rated reputation risk as "more important" or "much more important" than other strategic risks.[7] The reluctance to overhaul existing approaches to managing risk and reputation is even more surprising when you consider that board-level executives now regard damage to corporate reputation or brand as more important than financial impact in the event of a serious negative incident. The same Clifford Chance/EIU study found 57% of board members are most concerned about damage to reputation, 39% are most worried about the impact on share price, and 33% about the direct financial cost in the form of lost sales, a fine, or compensation.

Another reason that many companies have failed to manage the risks of social media comes down to a failure to understand the nature of the social web, to underestimate its power to harm, and generally to take too narrow a view of the risks. We saw in the last chapter how social media has a tendency to amplify existing risks, such as customer service complaints, the abuse of customer privacy through the disclosure of personal data, the release of proprietary and confidential information, or the abuse of copyright, trademarks, and other intellectual property. It is also modifying and changing the nature of these risks, for example by making political change more likely in countries dominated by autocratic regimes and weighed down by large young populations with many people out of work (see the next chapter for more insights into the societal and cultural threats of the social web).

KNOWNS AND UNKNOWNS OF THE SOCIAL WEB

In response to a journalist's question about the apparent lack of a direct link between Saddam Hussein's regime and terrorists seeking weapons of mass destruction, Donald Rumsfeld retorted:

> Reports that say that something hasn't happened are always interesting to me, because as we know, there are *known knowns*; there are things we know we know. We also know there are *known unknowns*; that is to say we know there are some things we do not know. But there are also *unknown unknowns* – the ones we don't know we don't know.[8] [italics added]

Rumsfeld's enigmatic statement attracted considerable attention, not to say opprobrium. What, people asked, was he trying to say? Or, more pointedly, what was he attempting to hide?

In addition to informing *The Unknown Known*, a 2013 documentary about Rumsfeld, his words have also seeped into corporate risk management speak. Just as a military force must consider carefully the different scenarios in which an enemy might attack, institutions or companies must think laterally about the threats that may confront them and prepare for the unexpected. One of the challenges of the social web is that it increases the likelihood of all three of these scenarios.

- **Known knowns**. These could take the form of established competitors using social media as a distinct point of difference, or high octane online discussions about carbon emissions emitted by your firm or your industry. In my experience many organizations already have some insight into established threats to their business or reputation by tracking news, information and discussions circulating online.

- **Known unknowns**. These are gaps in your knowledge or defenses that you know exist but are unclear how these threats may manifest themselves online and the extent of the damage they may cause. A known unknown could take the form of an smear campaign unleashed by a competitor questioning the competence or integrity of your leadership, or be about how likely an environmental group is going to attack you online and what form this attack will take.

- **Unknown unknowns**. These are the kinds of threats you know nothing about until they happen and when they do have a major impact. Al Qaeda's 9/11 attacks are a good example of an unknown unknown. This could also take the form of a highly disruptive new player in the marketplace – Nassim Nicholas Taleb cites Google as an example of an entirely unforeseen threat in his 2007 book *The Black Swan*; a more recent example could be Uber. Equally a green group working in conjunction with a little-known commercial hacker to expose your inner workings could be an example of an unknown unknown.

The social web also means that some direct threats to reputation have become much more likely and potentially far more damaging. As mentioned in the previous chapter, marketing and social media marketing campaigns can more easily run amok if they are seen as unprofessional, inappropriate, or unethical. Social media has also made it much simpler for competitors, angry employees, and irate customers and citizens to mount direct attacks on an organization's core business interests and reputation including through smears, slurs, protests and the threat of boycotts, sometimes causing significant damage.

Smear campaigns. Smears have long been used as a strategic weapon to undermine the credibility and damage the reputation of an opponent, particularly in politics. But they were more easily said than done; until recently, getting a slur into the public domain usually required professional help, a sympathetic media outlet, and perhaps a stuffed brown envelope. Nowadays just about anyone from a major competitor, aggrieved employee, or jilted lover can spread an unfair or untrue rumor and, thanks to their ability to do so covertly, they can be reasonably confident they will never be caught.

In September 2013, a video posted by an anonymous user purporting to show moldy jelly being prepared for sale at Hoi Tin Tong, a well-known Hong Kong-based manufacturer and retailer of herbal medicines, showed up on one of China's many online communities. Hoi Tin Tong hit back quickly, accusing a former advertising agency executive and supplier and now competitor of concocting the video. The retailer had a strong reputation but the video quickly went viral and the story was widely reported in Hong Kong's media, including the venerable *South China Morning Post*. Sales took a hit. But things got even worse a few weeks later when a government-backed study found that Hoi Tin Tong's turtle jelly signature product contained very little or no turtle shell. Whatever the truth, the results of both incidents were disastrous, leading to a significant slump in sales, badly damaging the firm's reputation and resulting in its CEO talking of having to shutter stores.

While many smear campaigns are anonymous, some take place in full public view. In December 2013, Chinese internet player Tencent posted a message on its Weibo profile accusing its rival Alibaba of planting negative articles about the instability of management at Tencent's Weixin (WeChat) subsidiary in the press and on a number of Chinese websites. Screenshots of the draft hit pieces, which had been crafted by a recently departed Tencent and now Alibaba employee, were also posted. Alibaba responded by accusing Tencent of running a similar campaign against it.

In another notable public spat in China, journalist Chen Yongzhou was found to have written 15 articles for southern Chinese paper the *New Express* alleging financial irregularities at construction equipment manufacturer Zoomlion, leading to a 9% fall in its share price. Further accusations were also posted on his blog. Yongzhou later publicly confessed to having been paid 50,000 yuan (USD 8,000) for his efforts and admitted that nine of the stories he submitted to his editors for publication had been given to him by a middleman. While the Chinese authorities have not named his backer, informed commentators reckon the plot was hatched by Sany Group, Zoomlion's top competitor, and was the latest salvo in a long-term feud between the two that included anonymous reports posted online two years previously accusing Sany of bribing government officials, allegations that had contributed to the failure of its IPO some weeks later.

Consumer boycotts. Consumers and the general public today have the power to hit you where you hurts. Social media is the perfect vehicle as you can recruit and mobilize large numbers of people, it costs next to nothing to set up and run a campaign and the impact can be huge. Most boycotts concern controversial products or services or plans to build factories that are seen to harm the local environment and communities. In an interview[9] for this book Ximena Beltran, formerly social media risk manager at US pharmacy giant Walgreens described how the drug retailer keeps its eyes peeled on online discussions about controversial company plans, policies, and products that might impact its financial performance and reputation. Walgreens' decision to launch a series of potentially controversial instant in-store blood-testing and genetic analysis labs in conjunction with Silicon Valley healthcare start-up Theranos is one example.

Boycotts – whether threatened or actual – can also damage a company's core interests. When Walgreens proposed to relocate its HQ to Switzerland to save taxes a public outcry ensued in the form of an activist campaign backed by over 200,000 people demanding that the drugstore does not "desert" the US, accompanied by the threat of a national boycott. Walgreens later backed down.

Mergers and acquisitions. Social media is also being used to mobilize opinion against controversial corporate deals. In 2010, online petitioners secured their first notable regulatory scalp after Rupert Murdoch's News Corporation had submitted a bid to take full control of broadcaster BSkyB, prompting concerns about concentration of media ownership in the UK. In response, global civic campaign groups Avaaz and 38 Degrees (a UK-centric campaign site with 2.5 million members) teamed up to pressure the British government, widely seen to have close ties with Murdoch, to refer the bid to a full review by the UK Competition Authority. Together the two collected and submitted 60,000 online "signatures" against the bid to the UK media regulator Ofcom, sent 50,000 messages direct to UK Prime Minister David Cameron and then Culture Secretary Jeremy Hunt and, following Hunt's announcement that the broadcaster's editorial independence would not be threatened by the merger, another 40,000 signatures to the Department of Culture, Media and Sport. The groups also arranged protests outside Parliament, bought adverts in *The Financial Times*, *Daily Mail*, and other newspapers, and issued three legal opinions on the need for stronger media rules. After some prevarication, the merger was officially referred to the UK Competition Authority and was finally withdrawn in the wake of the Leveson Inquiry into the culture, practices, and regulation of the British press after a phone hacking scandal at News International (now News UK), the UK arm of News Corporation. Jeremy Hunt confirmed during the inquiry that Avaaz's interventions had significantly influenced his decision on the proposed merger.

4

Social and Environmental Threats

In September 2011, not long after receiving USD 45 billion in US government bailout funds and two days before controls on debit transaction fees in the US were about to take effect, a memo disclosing that Bank of America (BoA) was on the verge of slamming a monthly charge of USD 5 on its local debit card customers was leaked to the *Wall Street Journal*. The news led to a huge outcry, prompting a number of newspapers to advise their readers to switch to better alternatives and to two back-to-back online campaigns organized by irate customers that culminated in an estimated 600,000 people transferring around USD 4.5 billion from BoA and its main street retail counterparts to community and credit unions.[1]

The backlash against Bank of America is noteworthy as it shows four ways societal issues and the social web are intersecting to make companies (and governments) more vulnerable: the emergence of activism as a mainstream activity; the transformation of activist organizations into more diffuse, amorphous networks; much less predictable lines of attack; and activists' ability to cause significant damage to an institution's core interests and reputation.

Online activism is the new opium of the people

Once operating largely in the margins of society, non-governmental organizations (NGOs) of different kinds have become increasingly numerous and widely accepted. According to *Wikipedia* there are an estimated 1.5 million NGOs in the US, in India there were an estimated 2 million in 2009.[2] While many remain local, organizations such as Amnesty International, Greenpeace, Oxfam, and the World Wildlife Fund (WWF) have expanded internationally and become increasingly powerful, holding governments across the world to account through what former US Assistant Secretary of State and Harvard University Professor Joseph Nye terms "soft power." They are also highly trusted. Public relations firm Edelman's annual Trust Barometers indicate NGOs are significantly more trusted than business, the media, or government both by the general public and "informed publics."

The rise of NGOs and the trust accorded them is remarkable when you consider that the great majority have little money and are constantly forced to raise funds and prove their worth. Which is where the social web comes in. In an interview for this book, former WWF Singapore Communications Director Sourav Roy argued that "social media has completely changed the game, meaning we can communicate direct with the general public, which can vote immediately with their wallets. The stakes have become dramatically higher."[3]

Examples of established pressure groups using the internet to force change are legion. A recent example: in 2013, Mars, Mondelez International, and Nestlé, which together account for 40% of the world's chocolate market, succumbed to pressure about unequal pay for women working for their suppliers in four countries in response to an online campaign coordinated by Oxfam under the banner of its "Behind the Brands" program. The campaign was supported by over 100,000 people worldwide.

However official NGOs and pressure groups had little to do with the campaigns mentioned earlier against Bank of America and the US retail banking industry. Molly Katchpole, a 22-year-old graduate student, part-time nanny, and BoA customer, led the charge by starting an online petition on Change.org arguing the fee was "outrageous" and calling on CEO Brian Moynihan to reverse his decision. Within a month over 300,000 people had signed up, 21,000 customers had closed their checking accounts, and the bewildered bank had retracted the charge. Meantime Kristen Christian, a 27-year-old LA-based art gallery owner and BoA customer organized "Bank Transfer Day," an online campaign encouraging people to move their funds from major banks to credit unions by November 5 (coinciding with Guy Fawkes Day/Night). Launching her campaign on Facebook, Christian quickly amassed over 80,000 supporters and is seen to have played an important role in persuading thousands of people to shift their money.

ONLINE PETITIONS: THE NEW INSTANT DEMOCRACY?

Signing one's name to a cause on an online petition site is now a mainstream activity and covers just about every aspect of life, from environmental protection and human rights to tax avoidance, fair pricing, and the provision of local services. As I write this book, the petition that has garnered the most signatures (over 2.2 million) on online petition site Change.org was an attempt to persuade Florida's Attorney General to prosecute the killer of Trayvon Martin, the 17-year-old African American fatally shot by notorious local neighborhood watch volunteer George Zimmermann. 170,000 people have signed a petition asking British Airways to stop selling trips to

SeaWorld in Florida due to the fact that it holds orcas captive for entertainment, 152,000 Canadians are lobbying Canada Post not to stop home mail deliveries, and over 365,000 people are pressuring US Congress to revoke the tax-exempt status of the National Football League. In the UK, an ongoing appeal for the Royal Mail to pay the pension of a deceased former employee has the support of 121,000 people, and 303,000 people are behind a petition to remove a *Sun* newspaper columnist for calling Mediterranean migrants "feral." Meantime in Hong Kong petitions are critical of a local bus company's new policy on folding strollers (483 supporters), another calls for another bus company to increase the frequency of one of its services (118 supporters) and someone is calling for the local authority to recycle waste responsibly (84 supporters). Why bother complaining to the powers that be, which are unlikely to take much notice anyway, when you can easily take to sites like Change.org and potentially have your way through pure force of numbers?

Katchpole and Christian's actions are by no means isolated. Fed up with large institutions and able to bypass formal pressure groups, startling numbers of people are now using the social web to take direct action themselves against their bank, local factory, or government. Change.org, which describes itself as "the world's platform for change" counts over 77 million members in 196 countries (62% of which are women) and sees some 700 petitions started every day. Avaaz boasts over 35 million members in 194 countries. There is hardly a day when I am not invited to support some cause or other through Facebook. Thanks to social media, activism, once limited to students, tree huggers, and political dissidents, is now the opium of suburban housewives and white collar workers across the world.

The emergence of amorphous activist networks

Until recently companies likely knew which groups were squaring up against them, whether or not they were likely to join forces, and had a decent idea of what was in store if they refused to meet their demands. With the number of pressure groups multiplying at dizzying rates, expanding across the world and disgruntled customers or hobbyist supply chain experts able to click Like or start a petition at the click of a button, it is now more difficult to know who is out to get you, what form their attacks will take, and whether their demands will strike a nerve and draw the attention of professional activists or the media, or be met with a resounding silence.

For example, in late 2011 Bank of America would have had good reason to have been more worried about the Occupy Wall Street movement then protesting against social and economic inequality and camped out in lower Manhattan than the prospect of two of its customers taking it on themselves to encourage a mass exodus of its funds. Like Molly Katchpole, Kirsten Christian operated independently and came up with the idea of Bank Transfer Day on her own. But she was able to take advantage of existing links she had with the Occupy movements in LA, San Francisco, and Portland to get early traction, encouraging them to mention her campaign on their timelines, post links to Occupy-related Facebook pages, and to download and print the fliers she had produced. Within days Christian's campaign Facebook page had thousands of followers. But the success she had persuading tens of thousands of people beyond the Occupy movement to sign up and to move their money was almost certainly partly due to the fact that the campaign was seen to have been born out of personal disenchantment and was not seen as directly associated with Occupy, giving it greater credibility in many people's eyes.

In another example, in 2008 a storm erupted over Nike's 10-year, USD 1.3 million deal with local authorities in Tokyo to rename Miyashita Park, which had fallen into disrepair, as Miyashita Nike Park. In return Nike was to pay for the park's upgrade and install two new climbing walls and a skateboarding area. However the plan, which had been negotiated behind closed doors with the local authorities, saw dozens of homeless people displaced and surfaced concerns about the perceived commercialization of public spaces, prompting a coalition of homeless support groups, artists, and anti-Nike activists to come together under the banner the Coalition to Protect Miyashita Park from Becoming Nike Park. Protests were organized and Nike's flagship store in the middle of Tokyo was picketed. But the heat was not limited to Tokyo or even Japan – activists from many other countries used the fracas to accuse the footwear company of slavery and low pay amongst suppliers and alleged discrimination against black employees, further stoking an already heated situation and piquing the interest of the world's media. Protests spread to other Nike stores around the world. Eventually Nike and the local authorities in Tokyo decided not to go ahead with the renaming program.

In both cases people operating outside "conventional" activist structures initiated the protests, making it far harder for BoA and Nike to know exactly where pressure would come from and what form it would take. Today it is best not to think of activists solely in terms of big-name pressure groups like Oxfam or Greenpeace but as coalitions of the willing and able, whose ranks and shape constantly chop and change as interest swells and recedes.

Less predictable lines of attack

As a rule of thumb the higher the profile an organization, the more widely it is seen to be unfairly protected by government or other vested interests, or the more it is seen to be actively engaged in controversial activities, the more likely it is to be taken on by activists. But with limited resources and facing increased competition for funds and the general public's attention, even the best known and most global campaign groups have to focus their fire and harness their resources efficiently. Accordingly they are constantly looking for new and imaginative ways of cutting through the clutter and getting their point of view across.

To date the principal targets have mostly been corporate brands – Nike as a company, rather than its sneakers or accessories, BP as a whole instead of its acetyls or petrochemicals businesses. And as we have seen with Nike and Bank of America, some notable scalps have been taken. However activists have also come to realize that consumers and the general public often know more about and have a deeper bond with products and brands than with corporations, that they love their Nike Air Maxes more than Nike itself, and are therefore a powerful tool whereby their owners can be taken to task.

Greenpeace's attack on Nestlé over its use palm oil is a good example of this new approach. In March 2010, the environmental campaign group launched a report claiming to show definitive proof of widespread deforestation of Indonesian rain forest for palm oil production. The multi-country campaign kicked off with activists dressed as orangutans clambering over Nestlé offices and was accompanied by a slick, highly emotive online campaign centered on KitKat Killer, a mock video advert featuring an office worker biting into a chocolate finger that spews blood over his keyboard. The reason KitKat was targeted was because one of its ingredients is palm oil; KitKat also happens to be one of Nestlé's most visible and global brands. Massive media coverage ensured and over 1.5 million people viewed the video, thousands of negative comments were posted to the firm's Facebook page, and over 200,000 emails were sent to the company. The incident resulted in the Swiss firm partnering with the Forest Trust to achieve "zero deforestation" by 2015. "Targeting brands," Greenpeace has said, "was like discovering gunpowder for environmentalists."

Another area of focus is supply chains: images of child labor or rotting factories in China or Bangladesh are a well-established weak link that can be used to force a guilty party to the negotiating table. Activists also know supply chains are vulnerable as they are difficult to manage effectively. As it happens the management of Nestlé had been working closely with NGOs such as the WWF (via the Roundtable on Sustainable Palm Oil) for several years, had already set itself the target of sourcing 100% sustainable palm oil by 2015, and was on course to hit 50% by the end of 2011. However the Swiss firm was little more than collateral damage: Greenpeace's principal target was in fact Sinar Mas, a low-profile, Indonesia-based, Singapore-listed palm oil supplier seen to be at the center of the deforestation. Nestlé was forced to sever its ties with the Indonesian company, which subsequently lost several other palm oil contracts.

Business partners are also being targeted, especially when they are high profile and are seen to have an emotional connection with consumers. In July 2014, Greenpeace launched an online campaign pressuring Danish toymaker Lego to stop selling Shell-branded Lego sets at petrol stations in 33 countries. The campaign took the form of a video parody of the song "Everything is Awesome" from *The Lego Movie* in which a pristine Arctic scene is transformed into an oil-drenched nightmare, ending with the tagline "Shell is polluting our kids' imaginations." Cleverly promoted through a multi-lingual website and using the #BlockShell hashtag, the video has now been viewed over 7 million times and the campaign has attracted over 970,000 online signatures. Lego has a very strong relationship with kids and young adults, making it a tempting target for the likes of Greenpeace when the toymaker is in bed with a company like Shell. But Greenpeace's real target was Shell; like Nestlé, Lego was mere collateral damage. In October 2014, Lego ended its partnership with the oil giant.

With small pressure groups and individuals also in on the act, companies and governments face many more potential lines of attack and social media is the weapon of choice. Global, viral, and cheap relative to conventional advertising and direct marketing, activists are deliberately exploiting the fact that in an increasingly global and commoditized marketplace companies are actively marketing themselves using social networks, hashtags, crowdsourcing, and other forms of open-ended "engagement". They also frequently delegate the management of their social media profiles to juniors and interns, leaving themselves highly exposed to low-level attrition warfare, surgical strikes, and large-scale incursions.

Large-scale incursions. In order to get their message across effectively, activists understand they need to create campaigns that get people talking about the issues and taking action. Like any good marketing program this requires good timing, a powerful central idea and compelling content. In an email interview for this book, digital activist turned social media consultant Tom Liacas cites Greenpeace as "by far and away the leader in digital pressure tactics" and highlighted its

> masterful use of social media to bring certain corporate players into very uncomfortable positions. They have excelled at storytelling (rendering a complex issue through a simple but gripping narrative), packaging (using high quality videos and images to communicate their cause) and content marketing (leveraging their content through their vast networks and often achieving true viral reach).

Greenpeace's assault on Nestlé over its use of palm oil is often regarded as the gold standard for internet activism. Like other activists, Greenpeace had long been using websites, video, and email to make its point. But against Nestlé it stepped up a level by producing the memorable and meaningful KitKat Killer video that directly connected the issue of deforestation with consumer purchasing and ensuring its production values were as strong as something produced by a top tier professional advertising agency. It also produced a series of campaign websites, each localized for different markets, and provided a series of badges that could be downloaded and used to show support. Furthermore supporters were encouraged to take to Nestlé's social media profiles and to Twitter to highlight the issue, and in Germany a wall of tweets mentioning palm oil and Nestlé streamed live for days from a truck parked on a public road outside the food giant's local headquarters in Frankfurt, providing a powerful visual backdrop for journalists covering the story.

Greenpeace is also a master at using parodies and hoaxes to gain attention. In July 2012 Greenpeace and agitprop duo The Yes Men combined to create Arctic Ready, a campaign intended to highlight Shell's activities in the Arctic, at the center of which was a near carbon copy of the oil firm's Let's Go global advertising campaign and corporate website. Only the site replaced Shell's somewhat dry, corporate, voice with one exclaiming it's excitement about the prospect of drilling in the Arctic and encouraging people to actively support its plans in the region. The activists also ran a contest whereby people could create their own adverts over Shell-branded wildlife photographs, with the winning entry published as a real ad on a Houston freeway. Arctic Ready was described as "a new landmark in the history of hoaxes" by the Poynter Institute.[4] We'll explore how Shell responded to Arctic Ready in Chapter 10.

KitKat Killer and Artic Ready were also notable for the degree to which they deliberately flouted Nestlé and Shell's intellectual property. The KitKat logo had been altered to read Killer and supporters encouraged to use it in place of their personal profile photographs and in their online comments, prompting the Swiss firm to threaten fans of its Facebook page that their comments would be deleted if the altered logos were included. And Greenpeace blatantly re-used Shell's logo and artwork during its Artic Ready campaign, setting up a fake website and several social media profiles in the oil company's name. In both cases Greenpeace's victims were being deliberately provoked into making a foolish or disproportionate response that could then be used against them in the broader battle for public opinion.

Low-level attrition warfare. Creative campaigns may be a good way to get the public's attention but the everyday reality of activism is that it can take months and years to get people thinking and behaving differently. Greenpeace's campaign against palm oil had been going on for years before it found what it believed to be incontrovertible evidence of systematic deforestation in Indonesia. The campaign to stop Shell and other oil firms from drilling in the Arctic has also been a long haul for Greenpeace and other environmental pressure groups. Persuading citizens to stop smoking is a never-ending exercise.

Activists can gain some attention by providing a useful store of materials that people can read, share, and use, and by making sure these are visible on search engines and social media. For example, the WWF uses a constructive, educational approach to raising awareness about the consumption of shark fin that focuses primarily on spelling out the benefits of eating sustainable seafood. Its website contains FAQs, leaflets, and a downloadable Seafood Guide and encourages restaurants and hotels to offer "ocean-friendly" and "Alternative Shark-Free Menus" featuring seaweed extract and other materials of a similar texture (texture being important in Chinese cuisine) and publishes a list of hotels, restaurants, and other organizations that have pledged not to offer or consume shark fin. And it uses the social web and hashtags such as #saynotosharksfin and #SOsharks to regularly remind people of the campaign, to highlight latest milestones, and to urge its supporters to take action. The campaign has been remarkably effective, with shark fin imports to Hong Kong, the industry's ground zero, plunging by 30%, and exports from the former British colony to China collapsing by 90% between 2012 and 2013.[5] But it had taken years of painstaking work to achieve this.

Surgical strikes. The fact that companies are actively using the social web to market themselves has opened a wealth of opportunities for activists to poke fun and make their case in a very public setting. Unless they are properly protected, it is far from difficult to hijack a company's social media profiles, something that has been done many times by activists. However a hijacked profile can be restored quickly; more damaging is when activists commandeer your latest marketing program or campaign to get their message across. Activists played a role in derailing Qantas' #QantasLuxury campaign; McDonald's attempt to get people in the US talking positively about its Happy Meals by paying to promote the #McDstories hashtag on Twitter[6] quickly became a touch paper for critics' and activists' concerns about the quality of its products. And the restaurant chain's #CheerstoSochi campaign encouraging people to celebrate the 2014 Winter Olympics (and its own sponsorship of the Games) was taken over by LGBT activists protesting a federal law in Russia banning "homosexual propaganda," leading to acres of negative media coverage.[7] Such opportunistic, surgical social media strikes are arguably just as effective, and massively cheaper, than preparing and running a costly creative campaign.

THE PERILS OF SOCIAL STANDS

Poverty, disease, sustainability, lack of access to clean drinking water, and a host of other issues provide companies with myriad opportunities to develop innovative products and make money whilst being seen to be doing good. Companies and charitable foundations pour money into worthy causes. Funding for "social entrepreneurs" abounds. Business is increasingly expected to play the role of an active citizen and help solve social issues.

However, these opportunities can be fraught with danger. Society is ever more politicized and the tribalism of social media increases the risk of social engagement being questioned or even attacked. Popular US restaurant chain Chili's Bar & Grill experienced a huge online storm as a result of promising to donate 10% of its "qualified" sales for a day during National Autism Awareness Month to the US National Autism Association. Why? Many of Chili's customers objected to the stance the Association took by not supporting vaccinations.

Organizations with a social purpose of one sort or another built into their DNA are also exposed to online pressure. US fast food chicken sandwich maker Chick-fil-A's stated corporate purpose is "To glorify God by being a faithful steward of all that is entrusted to us" and its outlets are always closed on Sundays. But it faced a massive backlash from gay rights groups and sympathizers when it confirmed on its Facebook page that it had contributed millions of dollars to Christian organizations opposing same-sex marriage.

Substantial damage to core interests

Campaigns such as Greenpeace's KitKat Killer, the World Wildlife Fund's slow-burn shark fin campaign, and the appropriation of social media marketing campaigns and profiles show creative, committed, and nakedly opportunistic use of the social web can cause real damage to an organization's business and reputation. Bank of America lost thousands of customers and hundreds of millions of dollars of revenue thanks to two online petitions. Shell lost a long-term business partner in Lego and millions of dollars of potential revenue due to a creative and smartly targeted online video.

In some instances the stakes are extremely high, jeopardizing the credibility and legitimacy of major institutions. The first real indication of the raw power of social media-fueled mass movements came in the toppling of the Egyptian, Tunisian, and Libyan governments during the so-called Arab Spring in 2011 and 2012. Social media was also central to the huge anti-corruption protests in India convened by social activist Anna Hazare. Corruption was seen as a major reason India voted to change government in May 2014.

The social web is also being used to threaten companies' license to operate. For Tom Liacas, much of the current discourse surrounding "social license to operate" (a slippery concept defined by *Wikipedia* as "a local community's acceptance or approval of a company. Social license exists outside formal regulatory processes. Social license can nevertheless be acquired through timely and effective communication, meaningful dialogue and ethical and responsible behavior") has come about as a result of the rising influence of peer opinions and activists' ability to mobilize opposition quickly through social media. "No longer can public powers automatically give the green light to commercial projects in the face of widespread opposition," he warns.[8] The debate over social license is centered on the energy and natural resources industries in Australia, Canada, Indonesia, and other resource-rich nations and has seen NGOs working closely with local communities threatened by mining and pipelines to raise awareness and, where necessary, mobilize opinion. We have already seen how social media was at the heart of attempts by Greenpeace to stop Shell drilling for oil in the Arctic. Activists and local communities now use Weibo and Weixin (WeChat) by default to halt the development of chemical plants in China.

However it is also easy to overestimate the power of online activism. Activist networks today may be large, professionally run and increasingly well connected but they can easily suffer from unclear and even conflicting objectives, as Hong Kong's Umbrella Revolution protestors discovered to their cost. And while some campaigns meet or even exceed their objectives, most fail to cut through the noise or convince the general public of their merits. Further more, while slacktivists (or "armchair activists", which most of us are), may click Like on a cause on Facebook or back a petition on Change.org, they are unlikely to do much more.

chapter 5

Behavioral and Legal Threats

Companies that behave badly or break the law have long been the stuff of media and public fascination. Often difficult to detect, it took time for the full extent of a problem to become public. However in today's ultra-transparent and networked world fraud, bribery, corruption, discrimination, harassment, sexual misconduct, and other forms of inappropriate or unethical behavior are much harder to hide and when discovered spread like wildfire. A study by law firm Freshfields Bruckhaus Deringer found that news and commentary about crises stemming from behavioral issues spread faster online than any other type.[1]

However the social web does not simply amplify these kinds of issues, it has also opened a Pandora's box of risks about how organizations behave on Facebook and other social media platforms. Some of these threats, such as employees mouthing off about their boss on Facebook or a firm misusing a third party's intellectual property, can result in significant negative publicity and, in some instances, lead to legal action. In addition there are a number of threats, including censorship, abuse of privacy, and defamatory attacks by aggrieved employees or competitors, that can cause immediate and deep damage to your reputation.

With the public now able to observe, comment on, and share your every move, much now hinges on how you respond online to behavioral and legal issues. Be seen to handle them quickly, openly, and proportionately and you'll win the benefit of the doubt; handle them unprofessionally or in an unreasonable or heavy-handed manner and you can expect a backlash.

Employees going AWOL in social media

"Done working for the weekend. Jazz fest time!" tweeted newly hired PayPal Director of Global Strategy Rakesh "Rocky" Agarwal after a day's work in New Orleans in May 2014. But things later took a turn for the worse when he took to Twitter to publicly insult a pair of colleagues, calling one a "useless middle manager" and "piece of s***" and calling for another to be fired. Realizing his error, Agarwal later deleted the evidence, apologized to his bosses, and blamed the episode on his new smartphone, claiming the messages were meant for a friend. He was promptly fired.

Until recently you could be reasonably assured that silly, inappropriate, or offensive things said by your employees stayed by the water cooler. No longer – the advent of Facebook and Twitter mean that rumors, allegations, and evidence of sexist, racist, or abusive colleagues and unkind, over-zealous, or unpleasant bosses can be made public instantly. Mercifully, however, deliberate attempts by employees to insult their bosses or colleagues remain relatively rare.

Arguably more challenging is the way social media has blurred the space between our professional and personal lives, resulting in a host of embarrassing incidents. The owners of Amy's Baking Company (Scottsdale, Arizona) responded to being humiliated on an episode of *Kitchen Nightmares* with British chef Gordon Ramsey by slamming their own Facebook fans variously as "REDSHITTORS" (aka users of the popular US social news community Reddit), "Pussies," "Punks," "Disgusting Pig People," and "Losers."[2] Staff at fancy Kuala Lumpur delicatessen Les Deux Garçons called their customers "bitches" in response to a complaint on Facebook about the quality of their customer service.[3] Both incidents resulted in a huge uproar and a welter of negative press coverage.

Employees publicly denigrating their bosses, colleagues, or customers on the social web inevitably leads to trouble. However some threats are rather less obvious. It was hardly surprising that Rocky Agarwal's rant went viral given the nature of what he said and that he let loose on Twitter. However there's also a real threat from employees behaving stupidly or making offensive comments that are totally unconnected with work on ostensibly private networks such as Facebook.

Understandably, employees figure they can say what they want to their friends using their personal social networks. But most personal online networks are dominated by loose ties – colleagues, former colleagues, and people we've met in the pub – as opposed to close and trusted friends, and it is easy to forget that their profiles can be indexed by search engines, meaning personal stuff now regularly makes its way into the public domain that not only makes the protagonists look foolish but which can also reflect badly on their employer.

PUSHING THE WRONG BUTTON IN SINGAPORE

You need only the length of the taxi ride from Singapore's Changi airport to the city center to appreciate that the Lion City is an uncommonly well-run place. Neat, tidy, and superbly organized, even the myriad trees lining the road appear choreographed to blossom year round. Singapore's transformation from obscure island off southern Malaysia to British trading post and, more recently, Asian tiger is well documented, as is the cultural conservatism underpinned by racial and religious toler-ance between the many races that form its population and which are seen to have contributed greatly to the tiny nation's extraordinary success.

In reality, racial tensions lurk below the carefully cul-tivated consensus. But it was still a shock when Amy Cheong, a Malaysia-born, Australia-educated senior exec-utive at top local insurance co-operative NTUC Income, took to her personal Facebook page in October 2012 to vent about what she saw as the local Malays' cheap, long weddings and high divorce rates:

> How many fcuking days do malay weddings at void decks go on for??? Fcuk!!! Pay for a real wedding you asshole, maybe then the divorce rate won't be so high! How can society allow ppl get married for fifty bucks? Kns!

The post was apparently leaked by a friend or colleague and led to a massive media and online backlash accusing Ms Cheong of racism. The incident also surfaced simmer-ing racial tensions across the nation, resulting in Singapore Prime Minister Lee Hsien Loong, various government ministers, members of parliament, and civic leaders pub-licly condemning Ms Cheong's actions and defending the local racial status quo. The incident also raised questions about the effectiveness of NTUC's 1,500 day "Cultural" and "Orange" Revolutions[4] launched by then CEO Tan Suee Chieh, campaigns aimed at transforming the traditionally conservative company into "a modern Singapore icon, a social enterprise of distinction" that would combine a reputation for strong ethics and trust with a more professional and dynamic approach to running its business.

There's also the risk of news-hungry journalists and bloggers on the lookout for examples of poor employee behavior to contend with. Where better to look than their personal Facebook pages or Instagram profiles? In May 2011, staffers at Australian advertising agency GPY&R awoke to articles in the nation's press detailing how their colleagues had been publishing "degrading" images of women on their personal social media accounts, describing then Prime Minister Julia Gillard as a "lesbian" and that their CEO was a member of the "Pippa Middleton ass appreciation society" Facebook group. A little obnoxious perhaps but hardly a big story; your average Aussie would barely blink at such goings-on. But the agency had just been selected to review the nation's Defense Force social media policy following a high-profile scandal in which a young recruit had broadcast himself having sex with a fellow trainee to colleagues over Skype, and journalists were looking for ways to extend the story. Given the project was not put out to tender, it is also possible that they were tipped-off by an envious competitor to GPY&R.

Aggrieved employees and former employees

In March 2012, Greg Smith announced his intention to quit Goldman Sachs in a withering op-ed in the *New York Times,* accusing the bank of having a "toxic and destructive" culture and placing greater importance on its own money-making than on its clients.[5] Smith's resignation came out of the blue and caused real consternation amongst Goldman employees and leaders, forcing CEO Lloyd Blankfein to publicly defend its culture and practices the same day. Whilst a public resignation is hardly a conventional way to part company, Smith was following a well-trodden path by using the mainstream media to inflict maximum pain on his employer. But not everyone can persuade the *NY Times* to run a sob story; rather Facebook, blogs, and employee review sites such as Glassdoor mean aggrieved employees can easily get their own back and, better still, they can do so anonymously.

Fortunately negative comments posted to Glassdoor and similar employer review sites are often ad hoc and while they may raise pertinent questions about a company's working culture, conditions, and pay, the impact on reputation tends to be minor, if incremental. Nonetheless employees are also becoming more proactive and cunning about how they use the social web, using pseudonyms and fake social media accounts to publish confidential information or to make serious and sometimes unfounded allegations about the way their employer is being run, or to cast assertions about the professional conduct or personal lives of their colleagues.

Some employees are also prepared to put their heads above the parapet and attack you in their own names. These incidents can be highly damaging if they have the support of their colleagues or the ear of senior journalists. In January 2008, Rudolf Elmer, formerly Cayman Island COO at Swiss private bank Julius Bär, passed details of around 2,000 individuals parking their money offshore in the Cayman Islands to WikiLeaks founder Julian Assange. The fact that he was passing the information to WikiLeaks, then a relatively little known entity, was a story in itself. That he did so by handing over the discs on which the data was stored at a press conference in London's Frontline Club only compounded the misery and led to a volley of very damaging publicity for the bank.

Taking on the top bosses at Japanese camera maker Olympus for an alleged cover-up of USD 1.7 billion (memorably recounted in his book *Exposure*), British businessman and former Olympus CEO Michael Woodford initially found it hard to convince Japan's highly conservative mainstream media to cover his story. And while he felt that most Olympus employees would support his case, he also knew that few would be prepared to voice their opinions publicly. So Woodford supporter and former fellow board member Koji Miyata set up Olympusgrassroots.com, a Japanese and English language website to petition for Woodford's reinstatement. On the homepage of the site Miyata appealed to Olympus employees across the world in the following terms:

> I cannot sit passively by and witness the demise of the company I love. My perspective outside the company affords an objective view of the depth of the crisis that Olympus faces. It also offers a glimpse of the very real potential for overcoming the present adversity. Please join me in expressing your support for concrete measures to revitalize the company we all love.

Miyata describes the site as "incredibly successful," attracting over 50,000 views in the first five days and thousands of supportive emails, many of which were published publicly. It was also instrumental in persuading Japan's mainstream media to take the issue seriously. Later, after an independent committee had vindicated Woodford and called for the Olympus board as a whole to step down, Miyata sensed an opportunity to cement real change at the firm and persuaded Woodford to do a live question and answer session on the popular Japanese online video network Nico Nico Douga, so that Olympus employees could ask him questions direct.[6] At the end of the session, 75% of the audience voted in support of the Englishman.

Woodford was ultimately thwarted in his attempts to be reinstated by Olympus' institutional shareholders in Japan, though he was eventually awarded a substantial out-of-court settlement for wrongful dismissal and defamation. Olympus was forced into strengthening its corporate governance and reducing its workforce; two board members and an auditor were sentenced to jail. In April 2014, several banks filed a civil suit for JPY 28 billion (USD 233 million) in damages.

Inappropriate, offensive, and unethical marketing

Whether TV based, on social media, or run across multiple platforms, marketing that is deemed to be offensive, nakedly self-serving, or opportunistic inevitably leads to a backlash. Tweets by shoe designer Kenneth Cole hijacking (aka "newsjacking") first the Egyptian revolution and then the prospect of American troops in Syria led to widespread accusations of shameless opportunism and tastelessness (he later claimed he was deliberately trying to cause a fracas).

> Millions are in uproar in #Cairo. Rumor is they heard our new spring collection is now available online at http://bit.ly/KCairo-KC.
>
> "Boots on the ground" or not, let's not forget about sandals, pumps and loafers. #Footwear

But there are also instances when the picture is less clear. On the social web one man's meat is another man's poison, making it difficult to anticipate how your latest ad campaign or video will be seen. For instance, ING Direct bank in Canada ran a TV advert in which a depressed man suffering from "RSP" (aka "Retirement Savings Plan") and unable to eat or sleep is cured by a visit to its website. But the company quickly started receiving emails and feedback through the social web that the advert was disrespectful to people with mental health problems, something it had not envisaged and persuading it to pull the campaign. We'll see how ING Direct managed this backfire in Chapter 12.

If discovered, unethical marketing in social media is also a sure trigger for trouble. This can take a number of forms:

- **Astroturfing**. Defined as "the practice of masking the sponsors of a message or organization to make it appear as though it originates from and is supported by grassroots participants,"[7] astroturfing is a long-established tool for giving the impression that a cause or campaign is on a roll. Long popular amongst political operatives, the social web means just about anyone can now set up a fake blog that looks like it is penned by your supporters, or pay others to plant positive reviews or smear competitors. Despite attempts to regulate astroturfing, the practice remains widespread. Chicago University data-mining expert Bing Liu estimates one-third of all consumer reviews on the web are fake.[8] The problem is endemic across Asia. In April 2013, Samsung was discovered to have paid Taiwanese students to post fake benchmark reviews of rival HTC's smartphones and to report that they were "always crashing." In March 2015, Singapore-based influencer marketing network Gushcloud was discovered to have been paying bloggers signed up to use its services to smear competitors to Singtel, Singapore's dominant telecoms firm (an initiative Singtel later disclaimed knowledge of) by complaining about their networks and subscriber plans.
- **Sock puppetry**. A sock puppet is a fake identity that can be used to ramp one's own products, defend one's name, or tarnish another firm or individual. Like astroturfing, sock puppetry has long been practiced by politicians furthering their agendas or authors reviewing their own books under pseudonyms, and has become mainstream thanks to the ease with which anyone

can disguise their identity on Yelp, *Wikipedia*, and many other popular social media services. In October 2013, *Wikipedia* blocked or banned some 250 accounts discovered to have been set-up to make paid-for entries. Companies advertising for people to post fake reviews are often found online. One openly promised: "All you have to do is copy the comments and place a five-star review for the business we ask you to place the review for – and that's it!"[9]

- **Censorship.** One of the prices of social media is that you can be criticized about anything at any time. Criticism can hurt, especially when it is made in front of hundreds or thousands of other people. But the onus is on organizations to take barbs head-on rather than turn away or, worse, delete or hide the offending comments. Yet surprisingly many organizations do just this. Volkswagen was caught deleting negative comments on its Facebook page in 2012, after Greenpeace had ambushed the car maker's friendly "Do you have any resolutions and what would you like to see us do more of this year?" New Year message by asking it to stop lobbying against climate change laws. Researchers at Harvard University estimate the Chinese government employs between 250,000 and 300,000 people – the so-called 50 Cent Party (or Army) – after the amount supposedly paid for every post that successfully diverts discussions away from sensitive topics or bolsters the Party line – to censor what's being said online within the Great Firewall.[10]

Once discovered, the blowback to unethical marketing is usually immediate and relentless. Research by the Chartered Institute of Marketing into levels of trust in online marketing in the UK discovered that 62% of consumers are skeptical about companies' online marketing methods, with only 20% reporting high levels of trust and confidence in what companies say about themselves online.[11] 47% said that if they found a company was manipulating online word of mouth, they would very likely change their purchase behavior and boycott the brand or company.

"BLACK PR" IN CHINA

Unethical online marketing is rife throughout Asia but is perhaps most widespread in China. In February 2013, leading Chinese business magazine *Caixin* ran a special report on the country's burgeoning "black PR" industry, discovering that the going rate for deleting a negative post was RMB 1,000–10,000 (USD 150–1,500) and RMB 100,000 (USD 16,000) for blocking a search term.[12] The report also found that black PR agencies routinely use persona management software that enables their staff to manage between five and 70 online identity accounts each, and that they are paid based on the number of posts they make that are not flagged by moderators of China's innumerable online communities. The report also detailed widespread use of fake government stamps used to frighten community moderators into pulling posts from the web. Another well-known tactic in China is a more classic form of blackmail: a PR or social media marketing firm uses its connections to place a negative article online and then approaches the subject of the post to have it removed – for a fee.

The impact of offensive and unethical social media marketing is not just reputational; in many countries it also goes against industry codes and contravenes a growing body of legislation covering false advertising and defamation. New York Attorney General A.G. Schneiderman fined 19 companies a total USD 350,000 for manipulating consumer review sites by using fake identities and by paying bloggers in Eastern Europe and the Philippines to write fake reviews. At the time of writing this book, Gushcloud has been referred to Singapore's Infocomm Development Authority for smearing Singtel rivals Starhub and M1. Samsung was fined USD 340,000 by Taiwan's Fair Trade Commission for its covert actions against HTC.

Abuse of intellectual property

Trademarks, copyright, and other forms of intellectual property have long been a trade-off between encouraging others to use, talk about, and advocate your brands and thinking, while trying to ensure that they are used in a way that protects their intrinsic value. But the social web has made the management of these assets much more challenging, partly as their use is more difficult to track, partly because of a deep-rooted online culture that believes that photographs, videos, logos, straplines, and designs – irrespective of their real owner – can be used, copied, remixed, and shared at will.

The social media web has also thrown up a range of new threats relevant to IP owners and for organizations marketing themselves using Facebook and other social platforms. These risks include:

- **Brand name squatters**. There's a danger of people "squatting" on a company or brand name on well-known or emerging social media platforms, typically in the hope that one day they will be paid off. They may also re-direct users to competitor sites, activist sites, or pornography.
- **Cybersquatters**. Anyone can set up in minutes a fake or fraudulent blog, Twitter profile, Instagram account, or Facebook page in the name of a company, brand, or employee. Often these link to sites or pages mimicking the target in order to collect users' email addresses or passwords.
- **Typosquatters**. Similar to cybersquatters, typosquatters take advantage of misspellings caused by common typing errors or foreign language spellings to direct people from major social media platforms to fake or fraudulent sites or pages.

There's also the threat of misuse of your trademarks and copyrighted materials to consider. With everything now available online and in digital format, anyone can now download, use, and share your logo, strapline, designs, materials, and products whenever and in whichever way they choose, despite the best efforts of initiatives such as Creative Commons to broaden the types of content that can be used or repurposed, or Digital Rights Management systems to restrict the use of music and other digital files.

In all these instances, the impact on your business can be significant, from loss of sales to increased costs tracking and managing these kinds of threats, up to and including litigation. Even more important is the potential damage to your reputation, though this will depend on a range of factors, including the motive of the squatter and the visibility and resonance of your brand, to the extent to which the threat or resulting incident is talked about online and in the mainstream media.

In most instances, the abuse of social media profiles has an indirect impact on reputation. However there are also scenarios when fake social media profiles can be set up expressly to damage your reputation, typically by impersonating your company, brand, or someone connected with your firm, or when your pages are hijacked by activists looking to make a point about you.

Of course IP infringements can just as easily be made by people in your company as by outsiders. With organizations increasingly using social media to communicate and market their wares, it is only too easy for your teams (and their suppliers) to use logos, images, and materials owned by others (or of celebrities wanting to protect their privacy), thereby infringing on their copyright. And unlike many other IP infringements, those by your own people have a nasty habit of angering people and resulting in a damaging public firestorm.

For example, fashion brand DKNY was found to be using photographs taken by *Humans of New York* street photographer Brandon Stanton in one of its shop windows in Bangkok, resulting in Stanton complaining on his Facebook page. But the backstory was even more damaging; it transpired that DKNY had approached Stanton some months previously asking to purchase 300 of his images for USD 15,000, an offer he declined considering the sum inadequate. DKNY subsequently acknowledged that an internal mock-up of his photographs had been used "inadvertently," apologized, and made a donation to a charity of the photographer's choice. But its reputation was in tatters: the incident was mentioned and shared hundreds of thousands of times online and covered by the BBC and the *Wall Street Journal*, amongst other outlets.

DKNY's actions attracted so much ire partly as it was suspected to have gone back on its word. But, rightly or wrongly, the incident also reinforced widespread fears about big companies taking advantage of smaller fry unable or unwilling to defend themselves, legally or otherwise. In a similar vein, Durex was caught plagiarizing a post by top Chinese blogger Labixiaoqiu without attribution, leading to widespread condemnation and prompting Durex to agree an out-of-court settlement and a gift of three years' worth of free products.

To be fair both Durex and DKNY moved quickly to apologize and were seen to do so sincerely, thereby avoiding even more anger. However a poor or disproportionate response can damage your reputation more than the transgression itself. We'll look at how Shell responded to an IP infringement in Part II, for the time being the difference in approach to responses to two parody Twitter profiles is instructive. My former boss Sir Martin Sorrell – rarely out of the papers and no stranger to controversy – is mercilessly lampooned on Twitter under the handle @NotSirSorrell for what some see as his obsession with money, disdain for creative work, and a willingness to launch below-the-belt attacks on his competitors. Almost certainly written by an industry insider, possibly one that worked for a WPP company, the profile has over 2000 followers and is quoted in industry blogs and by the mainstream media. But WPP has not attempted to have it removed, nor has it engaged with it publicly in any way. By contrast, the owners of the *Daily Mail* newspaper in the UK filed a subpoena against Twitter in 2012 for refusing to release the details of an unknown Twitter user whose parody handle @UnSteveDorkland made fun of Steve Auckland, then CEO of the Mail group's Northcliffe Media business. News of the subpoena leaked leading to a storm of vitriol and the media giant withdrawing its case.

Abuse of privacy

Stoked by stories of regular and widespread government snooping, hacks resulting in tens of thousands of credit card details, social security numbers, and private addresses being stolen, and a lack of understanding about exactly what Google, Facebook, and others know about you, privacy is now a hot topic for individuals and organizations. The social web compounds the problem, making it easier for employees to share private information about customers, colleagues, or even about themselves, thereby opening the way for hackers, trolls, predators, and others to dig around and cause trouble, putting their employers in the spotlight and jeopardizing valuable relationships.

At one level, the social web has contributed to a general sense that technologies and companies are becoming more intrusive and that one's privacy is being compromised. Marketing campaigns can target people on social media on account of their interests, age, location and behavior, the number of people following them, or because they appear to know someone important, criteria that many people do not realize they are making public, only to be pitched with a product or tip out of the blue.

In other instances, the threats are more specific. Abuses of privacy can be accidental, caused by an employee thoughtlessly revealing a customer's telephone number or email address on Facebook or Twitter or accidentally sharing something publicly instead of through Facebook's direct messaging function. These kinds of incidents are embarrassing but thankfully the damage tends to be limited. Far more dangerous if the act is seen as deliberate, as when a server at an Applebee's restaurant in St Louis posted a photo of a customer's receipt together with a complaint she had made about the size of the gratuity and her signature to social news site Reddit, on the grounds that she thought it was unfair and that "other users would find it entertaining." We'll explore how Applebee's responded in Chapter 9.

Defamation

Nineteenth-century Prime Minister Stanley Baldwin once described the owners of British newspapers as having "Power without responsibility – the prerogative of the harlot throughout the ages." From the moment controls on printing were relaxed in the late seventeenth century, Britain's tabloid newspapers excelled at mixing news and entertainment with blatant rumor, a good deal of it concocted by businessmen, con artists and politicians. Journalism may continue to suffer from a poor reputation, yet it is a much more professional and responsible industry than it was in Baldwin's day and outright falsities are far harder to peddle through its pages. However in social media the rumor-mongers have another, far more powerful tool they can use and abuse, one which enables them to start and spread a false allegation at the drop of a hat.

The rate at which companies and individuals are getting unfairly slammed is sky-rocketing. Research by Thomson Reuters found that defamation actions jumped 23% in the UK in 2014, with much of the rise attributable to social media.[13] In an interview for this book Chris Anderson, Co-Founder of Tampa-based Cyber

Investigation Services LLC described how his firm now receives over 4,000 requests a year requesting help to counter serious online assaults.[14]

According to Anderson, the bulk of whose work is in providing investigative services to law firms, the great majority of these attacks are made by aggrieved former employees, competitors, spouses, and lovers with an axe to grind against high-profile individuals (usually business people, sportspeople, celebrities, and musicians), though higher-level professional services firms such as doctors, physicians, and accountants, local service outfits such as building contractors and hotels and restaurants, and firms doing much of their business online, including e-commerce outfits, financial services players, and medical suppliers have increasingly fond themselves in the line of fire.

The techniques employed to publish and spread false reviews and allegations can be sophisticated. Typically they are published on consumer review sites such as Rip-Off Report, Consumer Reports, and Yelp, 'social' news sites such as Reddit, and major self-hosted blog platforms such as Wordpress.org, which allow reviewers to be anonymous or to use pseudonymous names and some of which do not verify email addresses. Careful attackers will also upload allegations from an internet café or public computer, thereby making it difficult to track the IP address to a single computer, and do so to servers hosted outside their country of residence or in countries known to make life difficult for investigators, such as some countries in the Caribbean. In addition, detractors may take comfort in the fact that major Internet Service Providers (ISPs) and consumer review sites receive thousands of removal requests every day and take months to process appeals. What is more, many ISPs and websites are less willing to deal with defamation and reputational issues than IP infringements, according to London-based media and defamation lawyer and now High Court judge Justice Mark Warby in an interview for this book.[15] And then there's the price and difficulty of libel actions. In addition to being notoriously expensive, defamation cases are also tricky to win, with laws in many countries favoring free speech. For example, the UK Defamation Act 2013 requires claimants to demonstrate "serious harm" or, in the case of companies "serious financial loss."

6

Operational and Technological Threats

In April 2014, US Airways publicly asked a customer asking for her feedback after she had experienced a delay at Portland International Airport. Unfortunately the customer service representative attached a lewd picture of a naked woman in a compromising position with a model airplane to the tweet. Immediately the internet erupted, some in fury but most in embarrassment and amazement. Many speculated about what could have happened. Was an irate employee getting his own back? Had the airline been hacked? The truth was more prosaic – a member of US Airways' social media team had been trying to flag the picture as inappropriate in its social media marketing management system but had mistakenly included it in his response.

If US Airways can draw any comfort from the incident it might be that the majority of social media meltdowns are not caused by unforeseen attacks by enraged customers, aggrieved former employees, or conscientious objectors but by day-to-day operational issues such as poor customer service, inadequately tended social media profiles, or poorly devised and managed social media marketing programs, most of which are eminently fixable.

Poor social customer service

As US Airways will attest, customer service now plays a crucial front-line role in shaping reputation. In fact customer care has always been important, it's just that complaints used to be handled over the phone, by email, or in person and rarely made it into the public domain. But nowadays anyone can whinge publicly through social media and if they are sufficiently angry, well connected, or imaginative, a delicate situation can quickly escalate into a serious incident and even a crisis.

There are all sorts of reasons why organizations are tripping up in this area. One problem is that many people believe that large firms are huge, faceless, and self-interested entities more concerned about the performance of their stock price than in dealing with people complaining about their products. There's also the fact that Twitter and Facebook are widely seen as convenient and effective ways of getting the attention of even the biggest and most faceless monolith, not least when someone has spent the last 20 minutes waiting for someone at your call center to pick up the phone. And the longer you take to respond – people expect an answer to their questions and complaints through social media immediately, and preferably within an hour – the more incompetent, uncaring, or evasive you appear, and the more likely they are to complain about you in public.

Typically online complaints are posted to a company's official social media profile or on Yelp, TripAdvisor, or one of the other top consumer review sites. But with many firms responding only to a small percentage of queries, even on their own profiles, customers are finding increasingly sophisticated ways of making them take notice. Escalating a complaint to Twitter is now a favorite ploy, partly as people have come to realize that journalists, bloggers, and other opinion-formers use it regularly and may pick up on their case. According to a source close to budget airline Air Asia, some 40% of unresolved queries and complaints posted to its Facebook page are subsequently placed on the micro-blog platform.

Some are prepared to go even further. We saw earlier how Hasan Syed bought advertising space on Twitter to pressure British Airways into making finding his parents' lost luggage a priority. In China, English teacher and entrepreneur Luo Yonghao made several complaints on his Weibo account about the door of a refrigerator he had bought from Siemens three years earlier not shutting properly. Imagining his was an isolated case, he was surprised to find hundreds of people claiming to have experienced similar problems. Luo again pressed Siemens for a response, to which the German firm responded with a formal statement advising customers experiencing problems to contact its customer service team. A few weeks later, after more complaints and taunts by Luo and others, Siemens issued another statement, this time pointing out its products fully complied with Chinese safety standards.

Dissatisfied, Luo threatened to smash up his fridge along with two others reported as defective in front of Siemens' headquarters in Beijing, a threat he carried out shortly afterwards in front of a phalanx of journalists, bloggers, and consumer rights activists he had tipped off, laying into the fridges with sledgehammers and later holding a news conference in which he called for Siemens to admit there was a problem and to issue a recall. He then published photographs and videos of the episode to his blog. Siemens subsequently admitted the fridge doors were faulty and apologized.

As Siemens, British Airways, and countless other firms have discovered to their cost, handling customer service complaints on the social web is about catching them early, admitting there is a problem (where there is one), and sounding human and empathetic at all times. It is also important to consider how well connected the customer is: as a rule of thumb, the more networked the customer the more damage he can cause. Something of an internet celebrity,

Luo Yonghao had tens of thousands of online followers and was well known in a variety of circles in Beijing and beyond. Siemens was doubtless aware of his profile but appears to have under-estimated his anger and his ability to mobilize others.

Dealt with quickly and openly, the great majority of customer firestorms die out after a day or two of negative coverage; very few turn into bone fide crises. But if a complaint does escalate into a full-scale crisis the impact can be devastating, especially if you are a small organization with limited resources. An example is Lemp Brewpub & Kitchen, a restaurant and micro-brewery in Gurgaon on the outskirts of New Delhi. In June 2013, a group of eight friends visited Lemp to try out the "Hawaiian Sunday Brunch" on offer on restaurant review site Zomato. Only the Hawaiian special turned out not to be avail-able as the chef was apparently ill, the food they ordered in its place was late, cold, and tasteless, and they were overcharged. Worse, when they complained they were physically threatened by the pub's owner and staff, prompting them to call the police. However, the police sided with the pub owners and hauled the group down to the nearest station for questioning, though they were later released. Disgusted by their treatment, the group took matters into their own hands by anonymously publishing a blog post[1] detailing their treatment, to which Lemp's owners responded by publicly threaten-ing the group with defamation (a threat they never carried through with). The spat took off online like wildfire and, as is often the case, the public sided with the little guys. The result: Lemp's online rating collapsed from over 3 to 1.2 out of a possible 5, customers deserted, and the pub closed a few months later.

Poorly devised or managed social media marketing programs

For many organizations social media is largely about using marketing and PR to get people talking about their swanky new product or service, be it through running blogger programs or social media campaigns or crowdsourcing creative ideas. There's no question that the social web offers tantalizing opportunities to reach new audiences and build deeper and more mutually beneficial relationships and when programs and campaigns are developed and run in a way that truly involves the user they can be hugely successful (think Old Spice's brilliant Think Like A Man, Man campaign in which former NFL wide receiver Isaiah Mustafa videoed answers to questions sent in by members of the public on Twitter and Facebook). Handled inappropriately, however, the social web poses significant risks. We have already seen how offensive and below-the-belt tricks are more-or-less guaranteed to rebound online if discovered. It is essential that marketing programs are relevant and are not seen as intrusive or overly promotional, focusing instead on truly adding value and nurturing long-term relationships.

Social media marketing campaigns should also not unnecessarily open organizations to public criticism about some aspect of their activities. In November 2013, J.P. Morgan flagged on Twitter that one of its top Wall Street dealmakers would be available for an hour the following day to answer questions from students and asked for questions to be submitted in advance using the hashtag #AskJPM. But the progam instantly went off track as thousands of people mocked the bank for its alleged role in the financial crisis.

Quick! You're in a room with no key, a chair, two paper clips, and a lightbulb. How do you defraud investors? | #AskJPM @jpmorgan #Anonymous

> I have Mortgage Fraud, Market Manipulation, Credit Card Abuse, Libor Rigging and Predatory Lending AM I DIVERSIFIED? #AskJPM
>
> Can I have my house back? #AskJPM

Six hours later, the bank backed out of its Q&A. #AskJPM back-fired as it failed to appreciate the breadth and depth of feeling against the bank. Similar to #QantasLuxury, J.P. Morgan had inad-vertently provided a public platform from which people could vent their frustrations and anger in large numbers.

Another oft-repeated sin is to promise much and deliver little. For instance, a social media campaign run by Domino's Pizza in Australia heralding a major revamp in its business – "Can you guess what our biggest announcement in 20 years is? It's a #gamechanger" it teased on Twitter – turned out to be little more than a new range of pizzas with premium toppings. The retribution was swift and brutal. "What a waste of my time" complained one member of the firm's Facebook page. "THAT's the big announce-ment???? Big bloody deal. What a let down" riled another. "You spammed us for over a week for this?? Fire your marketing team" @thesleepydumpling wailed on Twitter. But some went further. "Deleting my emails from Domino's as we speak. No more market-ing from them, or pizzas" thundered blackvulvan3.

Underestimating demand can also get pulse rates pumping. In June 2013, McDonald's offered a five-week Hello Kitty Fairy Tales pro-motion in Singapore, in which a new and unique design would be made available through its stores every week. But McDonald's had seriously underestimated demand for all the toys, especially the final and previously unseen "Singing Bone" toy based on a Brothers Grimm fairy tale, leading to huge queues of people outside its stories, near riots as stocks ran out, and an avalanche of complaints on the web and on its local Facebook page.

Social media automation

In many ways social media is a demanding medium: the volume of posts about you is huge, people are always asking questions, and you are meant to keep your audiences sated with a regular diet of fresh content. What is more, online discussions fail to stop at 5pm and restart at 9am, forcing you to work out how you're going to hit people with your messages on the other side of the world when you are in meetings, tucked up asleep, or on vacation. Requiring skilled hands and a human touch, it is also surprisingly time-intensive and costly to manage your presence on the social web. So the idea of automating the management of your social media channels is therefore a tempting one, enabling you to work faster and more efficiently by publishing your posts at specific times, responding to messages, and greeting people connecting to you online.

However things can easily go wrong. Autoreply bots can misinterpret information or reply to the wrong users – hardly a great way to kick start a relationship and often resulting in online complaints. Autoreplies also look like what are they are: cookie cutter solutions to a medium that demands a real human voice. In addition, scheduled tweets may end up being posted during an unexpected natural disaster or event, making you look unprofessional, inconsiderate, or uncaring. Guy Kawasaki, considered a social media guru and known for sending out barrages of tweets, received considerable criticism for continuing in the same vein during the Boston Marathon bombings in April 2013.

Campaigns that automate social media can also go astray. Coca-Cola had to withdraw a social media marketing campaign it launched during the 2015 Superbowl that invited people to respond to any negative tweets with the hashtag #makeithappy, which would be automatically converted into happy images using the ASCII character encoding scheme. Coca-Cola's stated objective was to "tackle the pervasive negativity polluting social media feeds and comment threads across the internet" but it hadn't banked on a blogger at Gawker, having observed a white racist tweet transformed into a cute image of a bee, developing @MeinKampf, a Twitter bot that tweeted lines from *Mein Kampf* along with the #makeithappy hashtag, making Coke's own bot spit out passages from Hitler's manifesto alongside pictures of cartoon characters, sunny islands, and pirate ships.

IT security

Today, just about everything – official documents, data, emails, and conversations – is digital and can be accessed anywhere and at any time and shared with consummate ease. As we saw in Chapter 5, an aggrieved employee can now easily cause serious damage to his employer by uploading confidential or proprietary information to WikiLeaks, information sharing sites like PasteBin, or its encrypted sibling ZeroBin.

It is also relatively easy for external hackers to find weaknesses in corporate IT defenses. Hacking may have been around since the turn of the twentieth century but it remained the preserve of mathematicians, cryptologists, and computer experts until the 1980s, when the first underground groups of teenagers started infiltrating the computer systems of telecoms operators and government departments, mostly for pranks or to avoid long-distance phone call charges. However today's hacker is a world apart: an anonymous, full-time professional with his own office, server, and ISP who steals and sells passwords, contact information, and credit card details to the highest bidder.

Largely dependent on malware ("an umbrella term used to refer to a variety of forms of hostile or intrusive software, including computer viruses, worms, trojan horses, ransomware, spyware, adware, scareware, and other malicious programs"[2]) and phishing ("the attempt to acquire sensitive information such as usernames, passwords, and credit card details (and sometimes, indirectly, money) by masquerading as a trustworthy entity in an electronic communication"[3]) to prise open a corporate firewall, many hackers now expressly target social media as it enables them to exploit weaknesses in human behavior rather than looking for vulnerabilities in increasingly complex though well-protected IT systems. The fact that so many updates to official social media pages and individual profiles are made via smartphones, together with the fact that many passwords used to protect access to these accounts are very basic and few people yet use two-step authentication, makes the social web especially vulnerable to so-called social engineering (sometimes also known as "soft hacking") attacks.

According to software security firm Kaspersky Lab over 20% of phishing scams on the web today target Facebook.[4] For example, hackers regularly target people with emails or notifications set up to look like they are from Facebook, Twitter, or YouTube, and set up fake mobile web pages that imitate Facebook's log-in procedure. They may also set up a fake Facebook page or Twitter profile in your name and encourage members of your firm to participate in fake competitions and promotions in order to get hold of their email addresses and credit card details. Another popular ploy is to register names on Twitter, Facebook, and Instagram ahead of their rightful owners and then divert their followers to fake websites, gambling, or pornography sites where their information is captured. Equally hackers may manipulate your social media team by pretending to be a business partner or another member of staff in order to gain access to your IT system.

Not every organization is equally at risk. In an interview for this book Greg Mancusi-Ungaro of internet risk protection and threat mitigation specialist BrandProtect said big name firms such as Sony, J.P. Morgan and US discount retailer Target are deliberately exploited by hackers not just because they are well known but also as they are largely trusted, making it easier to tempt people to click on fake profiles, notifications, or emails.[5] However, more often than not individuals are the real targets of data breaches, and their employers little more than collateral damage. Target was attacked in late 2013 not because its attackers wanted to bring down the firm or damage its reputation, but because they wanted to steal the credit card details and other personal information of its customers, some 70 million of which were affected. Nonetheless the company was hugely damaged by the breach, booking over USD 160 million in costs and leading to serious questions about how competently it was being run, culminating in the resignation of its CEO.

Sprawling, unkempt official social media presence

Organizations have reacted to more and more people taking to the social web by developing an increasingly broad formal presence on Facebook, Twitter, YouTube, Instagram, and other social channels. As a result they may now have a much better understanding of the expectations and needs of their customers and other stakeholders, have a ready-made route to reach them and a way to manage issues and crises more effectively. However, in an interview for this book James Leavesley, CEO of UK-based social media risk management platform CrowdControlHQ, warns the rush to develop a presence, run campaigns, and decentralize marketing and customer service on the social web has spawned hundreds of official and unofficial Twitter profiles and Facebook pages owned by a mélange of employees, former employees, and business partners that are time-consuming and costly to maintain and which can look and feel radically different in terms of the logos, graphics, language, and tone of voice employed. This, he warns, gives the impression the company either doesn't know what it is doing, doesn't much care about how it is seen, or is unconcerned about protecting its intellectual property.[6]

A sprawling social infrastructure is also difficult to keep interesting and relevant and can result in troves of inaccurate and out-of-date information. This increases the likelihood of complaints by users and makes it easier for activists and other detractors to cause trouble. It also means you are more exposed to legal threats should complaints not be reported in a timely manner (if you are in a regulated industry such as healthcare) or if misleading statements or testimonials by third parties are not promptly removed (an obligation in Australia). According to Leavesley, the proliferation of official social media profiles also leaves you more open to IT security threats. The larger the number of accounts you have, the greater the number of potential vulnerabilities, and the trickier the challenge of tracking their use and abuse, he advises.

Search engine automation

If social media poses a largely indirect threat to an organization's IT infrastructure and hence to its reputation, the configuration of search engines can impact reputation in a much more direct manner. Search engine threats manifest themselves in two main ways: by associating a company or brand with negative information as people type in their search queries, and by making negative news and commentary about it visible in the results of their searches. Both draw on signals in social media to a greater or lesser extent. The problem is that both processes are automated and

Google, Yahoo, and other search engines jealously protect their algorithms and frequently alter them, making it is difficult to dislodge negative information even if it is unfair, inaccurate, misleading, or defamatory.

The experience of Northern Irish retailer Robinson's Shoes is instructive. In October 2012, shoe enthusiast and blogger Jesper Ingevaldsson took to *Shoegazing*, a Swedish blog popular with men's shoe fans, to lament what he called the "worst online shopping experience with truly lousy customer service"[7] at the hands of the shoe retailer. Several weeks earlier he had ordered an expensive pair of shoes through Robinson's website, but they arrived two months late and quickly developed cracks on the toe caps. Advised to return them by post and wait for a new pair to be manufactured, Ingevaldsson asked for a refund, which he only received several weeks later after being forced to wait for the new pair, which never arrived.

The internet is crucial to Robinson's Shoes – around 85% of its business is online. But Ingevaldsson's review quickly shot to second place in Google's results for searches on the company's name, costing it considerable sales and proving impossible to dislodge. Eventually the retailer persuaded Ingevaldsson to remove the post on the basis that it was unfair for a single bad review to have such a disproportionate effect on its business. But Ingevaldsson retorted he was unable to delete it himself, so a compromise was arrived at whereby the title of the post was amended to read "Robinson's Shoes: Dispute and Subsequent Resolution" and a note added that the matter had been agreed to both parties' satisfaction. Two years later the review still ranks in the top five results on Google.

Robinson's may count itself lucky that Ingevaldsson's review does not appear in Google's "autocomplete" results – the tool that prompts users with keyword suggestions as they type their query into the search bar. According to *SearchEngineLand,* Google auto-complete "generates recommended keywords based on a combination of the volume of searches, mentions in social media and the amount of content on the web for a given term."[8] In theory, the results should be factual and timely. For example, at time of writing if you enter "Barack Obama" into Google.com you are presented with "Barack Obama twitter," "Barack Obama facts," and "Barack Obama daughters" as predicted search keywords – none of which is going to cause much trouble.

However autocomplete also provides suggestions that can negatively shape behavior (by sending people to negative news and information) and perceptions (by reinforcing negative views and stereotypes). For example, type "BP" and Google's top recommendation (at the time of writing) is "oil spill"– a clear reference to the 2010 Deepwater Horizon blow-out. While unhelpful this will hardly bring down a firm BP's size. More damagingly, autocomplete also makes suggestions that are based on misleading and, in some cases, untrue information. In 2012, an unnamed Japanese man took out an injunction in Japan against Google when he discovered that searches on his name linked him with serious crimes he said he had not committed. As a result he was fired from his job and claimed he was unable to convince potential employers that he was innocent. Despite losing the case, Google refused to alter its search results on the grounds that they were generated automatically, did not violate his privacy, and because it was not regulated by Japanese law as its servers were housed in the USA.

* * *

The threats of the social web are wide ranging and differ dramatically depending on the company, industry, and the local social, political, economic, and media context. Understanding the landscape, conducting round-the-clock vigilance, and having strong defenses are critical to maintaining a strong online reputation.

Much also depends on how you are seen to respond, something that has become much more challenging when you are expected to move at light speed while simultaneously being open and honest. By looking at examples of organizations responding effectively and ineffectively, the next part of this book sets out how some of the more common threats outlined above can be managed.

part II

Managing Incidents

7

Formulating the Right Response

Despite your best efforts to be fully prepared, sooner or later one of your products is going to prove faulty, your customer care team will mishandle a complaint, a colleague will do something silly on Facebook, or an important blogger will say something unpleasant or untrue about your company. If you've prepared properly chances are you will be able to sort out these kinds of problems before they flare up into more serious incidents or even, God forbid, crises.

How you respond to incidents on the social web is similar in many ways to responding through traditional media. In both cases it pays to be alert to the situation, responsive, honest, and measured. But social media is also different in some important ways. While you are likely to know the journalist asking questions about your financial performance or have access to basic information about the customer complaining about one of your products, there's a strong chance you'll have never heard of most of the people you find yourself having to deal with online. And then you are expected to enter into public conversations and the unpredictable nature of the social web makes it difficult to know how your response is going to be received.

With research studies showing people expecting an answer to their enquiries and complaints on social media in minutes rather than hours, it is important you move quickly. And the pressure ratchets as you realize the longer it takes to formulate a response the more likely it becomes that their frustration will turn to anger, and that they are going to make it their business to pile on the pressure in public. Yet it is essential that you keep your head and don't overreact. As Ed Hoover, senior manager, crisis and consumer care at Mars observed in an interview for this book, "In my experience, many managers, sometimes even seasoned communications professionals, see negative comments or a flare-up on social media and think, 'WE MUST DO SOMETHING NOW!,' which could lead to an overreaction that makes it worse. Speed is king on social media, but it's helpful to pause before engaging and really think it through."[1]

Assessing the situation

It is often said that social media suffers from too much noise and little genuinely useful signal, making the job of assessing whether something is worth responding to and how you should respond to it a tricky proposition. But things are not made any easier by a tendency to see social media data as an end in itself, a game of numbers rather than a mosaic of interests, expectations, and intentions. Rather data should be seen chiefly as a weapon to identify and flag potential issues, track things as they develop, and to gauge the reaction to your response. It is worth paying close attention to the following:

- **Visibility**. The number of times a grievance is mentioned in online discussions and the visibility of the channel(s) on which it is circulating.
- **Virality**. The potential of a grievance to go viral based on who is interacting with it, where it has spread to, and its format and shareability. Video and photographs travel particularly fast online.

- **Sentiment**. How negatively a complaint or allegation is viewed online. Thankfully most social media listening systems enable you to gauge sentiment through automated natural language processing algorithms.
- **Influence**. The relative influence of someone based on the number of people following them and their credibility or authority on the topic in question (typically based on the volume of interactions with what they say or do online).

Fortunately these kinds of metrics can be tracked using most decent social media listening tools. Better still, the more sophisticated tools enable you to set up thresholds at which alerts are automatically sent to your social media listening team or the relevant pre-determined business unit. Thresholds can be set at different levels based on a combination of sentiment, volume, and influence and the relative severity of each threat, for example:

- **Severe**. An allegation of product contamination by a well-known journalist or blogger.
- **High**. An escalating rumor about a controversial product ingredient.
- **Moderate**. Ad hoc complaints about your products or services.

See Chapter 14 for a more detailed example of how to classify threats to reputation.

THE LIMITATIONS OF SOCIAL MEDIA LISTENING

Social media listening tools are invaluable for identifying and tracking potential problems. But they should also be treated with some caution. For a start they often fail to give a comprehensive picture, a problem when issues can easily emerge on the most unlikely channels. And then indicators such as sentiment analysis are often inaccurate (typically only 60–70% reliable), especially, according to founder and CEO of Shanghai-based social business intelligence firm CIC Sam Flemming, in a tonal language such as Chinese where a single word can have many more meanings than in a non-tonal language.[2] Online influence is also notoriously ill-defined. Klout, perhaps the best known online influence tool, ranks influence largely on the degree to which people respond, share, or mention what someone says or does online. But it ranked Justin Bieber as more influential than Barack Obama and the Dalai Lama, suggesting influence means different things to different people.

Sentiment, visibility, and influence are useful starting points for a deeper, more qualitative investigation into the potential impact of a threat and how it should best be managed, based on factors such as whether it is deliberate or accidental and is being made directly or indirectly. You should also consider the background of the individual or organization making the complaint or allegation, understand why they are complaining, assess whether the gripe is fair, determine how willing they are to co-operate with you, and gauge how likely they are to escalate the issue publicly. You might also want to consider where the customer or detractor is located geographically and whether the complaint is being made on one of your own channels or on an influential third-party channel.

Some threats will require a deeper understanding of the motivations and capabilities of your detractor. For instance, an assessment of an attack by Greenpeace or Friends of the Earth will require a good understanding of its motive and objectives, an appreciation of its campaign techniques, and a clear view of how much damage you are prepared to suffer. On the other hand, anonymous or pseudonymous defamatory attacks make it hard to know who is making the allegation and what their objectives are, meaning you will need to identify the IP address of your assailant to be in a position to understand their motivations.

Weighing your response

Just like traditional media, social media should not be approached as a magic wand that when waved in the right direction is suddenly going to make your problem go away. Quite the opposite – the social web means you are now more exposed than ever if people think you are being dishonest or trying to spin your way out of a situation; which makes it even more important that you fix the problem if you're at fault.

Sometimes, however, the cause of the problem is unclear and given the speed at which bad news now travels, you may not have time to fix it before all hell breaks loose. Conventional wisdom is that you should quickly acknowledge the issue and promise to get to the root of it. Yet the unpredictability of the social web means careful listening and good judgment is required to select the best response. Mars' Ed Hoover cautions, "Will our responding only fan the flames? 'Riding it out' can be a valid strategy in some instances. But it can also spiral out of control, so it's always a judgment call as to what the threshold is and when you need to jump in."

Five response options

There are five main ways you can respond to an online threat:

1. **Communicate**. Most negative situations demand a public response of one form or another, from a brief acknowledgement that you are aware of the problem and are trying to

resolve it, to a full public statement. Naturally your response will depend on the nature of the complaint or threat, but generally the more open, honest, responsive, and constructive you are seen to be, the better. As a general rule of thumb, if the complaint is legitimate you should own up, explain where you have gone wrong and what you're doing to fix the situation and, if appropriate, apologize. This usually takes the sting out of the situation. Where the picture is less clear, state that you don't have the facts but are treating it seriously and will revert as soon as you have something more concrete to say. And you should seek a retraction or publicly rebut clearly misleading or false statements – ideally on the channel where the problem first surfaces or, if this is not possible, using your own channels.

2. **Negotiate**. Finding a compromise by offering customers a refund, upgrade, or discount is often a good way to resolve an issue, especially when it appears legitimate. However in other instances, such as when a complaint or allegation appears questionable or where the issue being raised is a complex one that cannot easily be explained online, a more protracted discussion is required. In such cases, the best way to arrive at a mutually satisfactory conclusion is to negotiate offline, ideally face-to-face. Not only does this send a clear message that you care about your relationship but it will also reduce the likelihood of the complaint being escalated in public. Nonetheless you'll need to make sure that you are seen to negotiate in good faith and not merely as an attempt to take the issue offline and out of the public glare.

3. **Leave**. Some people argue that every negative statement, comment, or complaint about you should be responded to. Others say leaving them alone is tantamount to burying your hand in the sand. But there are also occasions when a situation is very volatile and you only stand to make matters worse by diving in, in which case you are better advised to hold off and watch and wait. In instances where an allegation about you is clearly unfair

or your detractor appears only really interested in provoking you, the community may well come to your defense. If you do decide to leave it or wait, you should track interest in the post for a few days to see whether it escalates, slows, dies, or mutates.

4. **Minimize**. When times are tough, the community is jumpy and people are breathing down your neck for answers, it is tempting to try and bury the problem by pushing an offending item down your Facebook page or off the first page or two of Google. Publishing new content can help distract people and all it takes is the creation of a few new posts to push something down Facebook. Conversely, minimizing the visibility of negative information on search engines typically takes a long time, the costs are considerable, and, as often as not, the results are disappointing, not least when Google changes its algorithm and you are forced back to square one. You should also bear in mind the risks of being caught burying bad news, which inevitably results in mayhem online and often leads to negative media coverage.

5. **Remove**. In certain circumstances, such as where a competitor, disgruntled customer, or former employee is making false allegations or posting fake reviews, you may want to take more restrictive action to defend yourself. Most of the major social media platforms now enable you to report fake accounts and copyright infringements or apply for the removal of offensive material. In Europe, you can also appeal to Google to delete "irrelevant" or "inadequate" links under the EU's Right to be Forgotten ruling. Equally you can consider your legal options, ranging from issuing a cease-and-desist notice against your attackers to requesting that the ISP, website, or social platform on which the allegation is posted surrender the IP or email address of your detractor. Ultimately you can also resort to arbitration or litigation.

Which of these five options or combination thereof you choose will depend on the nature of the threat. Many social media threats are minor concerns that can be dealt with quickly and easily by your social media, communications, or marketing teams and only require the use of a single option. Others are more complex and potentially damaging and may require a multi-pronged approach that carefully weighs the potential impact of the threat against the benefits and risks of responding in different ways.

Being reasonable and proportionate

Whichever route you choose, it pays to apply a light touch to negative situations on the social web. Much hinges on your tone. Coming across as professional, helpful, and humble counts for a lot and means people are much more likely to give you the benefit of the doubt. It may also mean they actively come to your defense if they reckon you are being wronged. Conversely people quickly take offense at firms that are threatening, dismissive, or rude. Having a light touch is also about being reasonable and doing the right thing, as opposed to being seen as preoccupied with protecting your reputation. Moving quickly to accept responsibility when appropriate and being seen to do everything in your powers to sort the problem out will persuade people that you are acting in their best interests rather than your own.

Sometimes, of course, you have little option but to use force, but your response must be seen as proportionate. We saw in Chapter 5 how attempts to suppress information online can easily backfire, thereby propelling a previously little-known issue or dispute into full public view – the so-called 'Streisand effect'. In other instances, while a legal threat may be legally or morally justifiable, it can also appear heavy-handed and like you are desperately trying to close the stable door after the horse has bolted.

Five common social media incidents

The social media landscape is littered with examples of organizations making a hash of their responses. We've already seen a number in this book. Of course, there are also many examples of organizations responding effectively, it's just that we rarely hear about them as they don't escalate into serious public problems. While each incident is different and requires its own solution, there is also an emerging playbook of principles and practices covering some of the more common negative incidents in social media.

Five of the more common threats include:

- **The Furious Customer**. The customer who, frustrated and fed-up with not being listened to or feeling she is being treated badly, turns to the web to vent her anger.
- **The Rogue Employee**. The member of staff who goes AWOL in social media, embarrassing your firm and raising questions about its competence, values or culture.
- **The Committed Activist**. The campaign group intent on highlighting through social media what it sees as your poor approach to environmental, social, or political issues.
- **The Hostile Journalist**. Coverage about you by a mainstream media journalist or big name blogger that is inaccurate or unfair.
- **The Backfiring Campaign**. Your marketing or social media campaign goes astray, leaving you looking tone-deaf or silly.

* * *

Staying calm, carefully assessing the situation, and identifying the appropriate response sounds straightforward enough in principle. But the social web can be an intimidating proposition when the crowd sees red and your boss is on your back. In the next five chapters we'll explore how companies responded to the five scenarios above to draw out some best practice principles and techniques based on where things went right and where they could have gone better.

8

The Furious Customer

However good your products or services are, there are going to be times when things go wrong. Your product is faulty, your customer service slips up, your online booking engine develops a glitch, or a customer is underwhelmed by what she thought was going to be a truly unique and special experience. These are facts of life even for companies known for treating their customers superbly.

Customers expect you to do what you say and respond imme-diately when things go wrong. More problematically, they have immediate access to all manner of powerful tools with which they can take you to task publicly if they feel you're not listen-ing. You'll recall how Hasan Syed bought USD 1,000 of Twitter adverts to shame British Airways into sorting out his parents' lost luggage. And how Ryan Block recorded a Comcast customer service representative trying to stop him cancelling his account and published the audio file online, later dredging up evidence of how the media firm used "Retention Specialists" trained in all manner of underhand techniques to dissuade customers from going to rival services.

In each case, the offending companies were caught napping – their responses were too slow – when the response was eventually made it was deemed insufficient or insincere. Speed is certainly important when it comes to handling customer complaints in social media but, as we'll see from how FedEx handled an irate customer, it is by no means everything.

FedEx delivery man goes AWOL

In December 2011, a few days before Christmas, FedEx PR manager Shea Leordeanu awoke to find a Google Alert in her inbox mentioning a video on YouTube apparently showing one of her colleagues throwing a package containing a PC monitor over customer's fence.[1] While there had only been a few hundred views, gut instinct persuaded Leordeanu that the video would go viral, and she and her team quickly set about dealing with it.

FedEx felt it could not respond publicly until it was satisfied the video was genuine, the customer had been identified, and the issue resolved. First they had to identify the customer. This was not straightforward – the house number was not visible and it was impossible to make out the number plate of the driver's van. The incident could have happened almost anywhere in the world but there were one or two clues suggesting it may have taken place somewhere on the West Coast of the US: the sun was out and the driver was wearing shorts (it was December) and the grass was in perfect condition. The team's hunch turned out to be correct, but it took 24 hours to identify and connect with the owner of the video, during which time their worst fears had materialized: the *Mail Online* in the UK had picked up on growing buzz about it and run a lengthy and damaging article.[2] Within 48 hours the video had been viewed over 3 million times and had attracted over 10,000 comments, many of which were incredulous or scathing.

As soon as the FedEx team had verified the video was genuine, it acknowledged the situation publicly by posting to Twitter:

> We saw the video and quite frankly were shocked. This was careless treatment of a customer package by our courier and will be addressed. 1/4
>
> We take pride in the quality of service we provide to millions of customers daily. 2/4
>
> We will not tolerate any irresponsible act that affects the quality of any item we deliver. 3/4
>
> Such irresponsibility is contrary to the good reputation FedEx is known for worldwide. 4/4

Having negotiated a solution with the customer, FedEx responded a few hours later through a video statement posted to YouTube and to its corporate blog featuring Matthew Thornton III, the SVP of US Operations at the firm's Express unit.[3] Thornton apologized, confirmed that the issue had been resolved with the customer and that disciplinary action was being taken against the relevant employee. He also tried to reassure readers that this was an exceptional case and would not happen again.

Key considerations when dealing with customer complaints in social media

Move fast but make sure of the facts

One of the biggest challenges facing organizations today is the speed at which they have to respond to online complaints. However this is far from easy when the facts are unclear. FedEx quickly understood the video was potentially damaging but it took 24 hours to identify the owner of the video and to acknowledge the situation. It then took several more hours to issue a full public statement. With many customers now using Twitter and other channels to make and escalate complaints, you might think 24 hours is too slow – ideally a complaint should be acknowledged more or less as soon as it is made and responded to within 6–12 hours maximum.

Six hours is not much time to get to the bottom of what may be a complicated issue. But making sure your facts are straight and that everything you say publicly is factual, credible, and can be supported is essential – nothing irritates an already frustrated customer more than an organization speculating about what may have happened, seen to be getting the facts wrong – accidentally or deliberately – or having to get involved in a drawn-out discussion on Facebook that is leading in the wrong direction. And irate customers and bloggers love to poke holes in inaccurate, wooly, or cagey responses.

This is where an upfront acknowledgement of a problem can really help: a brief message saying something along the lines of "We're very sorry to hear of your experience; as our customer you mean everything to us and we are doing everything we can to get to the bottom of this" will reassure your customer that they are being listened to and that you are on top of things. But it will also buy you time to start the process of finding out what has happened, what you should do about it, and to address the issue in public more fully.

Of course, a single brief acknowledgment of an issue is not necessarily going to get you off the hook on every occasion – some customers are looking for an immediate and full response, come what may. But while it might be tempting to say something to get them off your back, most people will accept it if you simply say you don't yet have the full facts, you're doing everything you can to help them, and will revert as soon as you can.

Do the right thing in the right way

Nobody likes criticism, especially when it is harsh, strikes a chord, and when the eyes of the world are on you. And when we are at our most vulnerable, our natural instinct is either to turn away, respond curtly, or to make rash promises in the hope that the problem is going to vanish. But running away only makes it appear as if you've something to hide, and a knee-jerk reaction can easily make you appear defensive or even paranoid. And while it can be tempting to play to the galleries by making a quick promise or apology in the hope that things settle down quickly, these can easily be interpreted as insincere. Or the facts may turn out to be quite different to what you expect, forcing you into an embarrassing U-turn.

While social media can appear an inherently volatile and hostile environment, it is usually also one that rewards organizations that are seen to do the right thing rather than being preoccupied with saving their own skins. To its credit, FedEx agreed to buy its customer a new monitor, irrespective of the damage and cost, and waited until it knew the facts of the case and the expectations of its customer before appeasing the online furor with a public statement. This was a brave call but one that eventually earned it the respect of its community.

It also pays to be careful about *how* you go about fixing the situation. FedEx chose to try to do this face-to-face with the customer, an approach that implied it truly cared and which gave it the opportunity to build a stronger relationship with the customer going forward. (Worth noting is that the individual concerned has not complained publicly about the incident since it happened even if the video remains online where he posted it and has now been viewed over 9.5 million times.) Yet sometimes it is not possible to resolve customers' complaints by meeting them in person or taking the process offline: they may be far away or do not have the time to meet you. In other instances, they may want you to suffer publicly. In these scenarios you are going to have to resolve the situation in the open, which requires careful attention to your tone and deft handling of the mechanics of your interactions. With nerves strained, it is critical that you are seen to understand the issue, you are open and sincere in trying to find the right solution, and that you are always polite and professional, accepting criticism where it is warranted. And then it is important to get the small details right. If you need to ask a customer to share their contact details with you, make sure they are following your Twitter feed if you want them to direct message you. If you want them to telephone you, make sure you give them a local, or better still a toll-free number rather than an expensive overseas number.

There's another benefit to being overtly reasonable and open in how you respond: customers or members of the community who are being explicitly unreasonable will quickly come across for what they are. In my experience, you are rarely backed immediately when something negative happens to you. But if your community believes you are genuinely trying to do the right thing, only to be rebuffed by those more interested in themselves than others, it will almost invariably come to your side.

Be seen to be listening and learning

It is tempting to think of a negative incident as something that needs to be resolved as quickly as possible. But it can also be a valuable opportunity to understand where you went wrong and how you can improve. Matthew Thornton III's video message drew well over 100 comments on the firm's corporate blog and almost 1,500 comments on YouTube, many of which were supportive of the firm and of what they saw as Thornton's heartfelt and appropriate response. However there was also a visible minority of skeptical and outright critical commentators asking why the employee was not fired and whether the episode was symptomatic of broader problems stemming from an ongoing cost-cutting program. FedEx made no attempt to respond to these allegations or appear as if it was listening to constructive criticism.

At the very least, you should have a close look at people's comments and see if there's anything you can learn from them – there often is. But you can also use a slip-up as a chance to go beyond the PR pleasantries and demonstrate publicly that you care about your customers and are set on learning from what they've got to say. A great way to do this is not simply to make a public statement and move on, as FedEx appeared to, but to participate in the conversation on an ongoing basis, thanking people for their suggestions, probing deeper when someone says something particularly insightful or valuable, acknowledging issues you are aware of, and asking how you can do better. Sure, some people may take advantage of your vulnerability and the fact that you are willing to listen and engage as an opportunity to kick you when you are down. But many more will realize you are sincere in your intentions.

You don't need to respond to everyone

Given that complaints on Facebook or Twitter can go viral at any moment, it is tempting to think that everyone and everything negative should be responded to. There's plenty to recommend this approach – after all, your customers should be treated equally. Firms that top the lists for good social customer service like KLM, Orange, and Indonesian mobile phone operator Telkomsel, consistently respond to well over 90% of questions and issues raised on Twitter or Facebook, and in some instances over 99% of cases.

However sometimes you may find yourself unable to answer everyone's grievances, as someone is sick or on leave or because your team is insufficiently resourced at the best of times. Depending on the volume and nature of the problems, you may want to focus on those that appear most credible or require the fastest action. And while in theory all customers are equal, there's a strong case to be made for prioritizing customers, bloggers, or journalists with tens or hundreds of thousands of followers, especially those with reputations for objectivity and known to have a low opinion of your company.

You'd also do well to remember that all is not what it appears online. Some people may not be customers at all but scammers trying to extract a freebie or extort money. "Complaints" of this nature need to be treated carefully. In these instances there's a strong argument for not responding as you may only inflame the situation, thereby giving the customer the credibility or visibility they crave.

Take control when appropriate

If there are good reasons to be cautious about whom you respond to online during a difficult situation, there may also be occasions when you have little option but to put your hat firmly in the ring. Things can easily get heated online, resulting in slanging matches between your customers. You may find yourself being provoked by a customer or troll and get into a heated argument. Or a customer, for whatever reason, may end up threatening or revealing the personal details of one of your people. Allowing this kind of behavior will only make an already difficult situation worse and, in some instances, may leave you legally exposed. So it is very much in your interests to step in and make sure everyone is behaving within the parameters of acceptable behavior.

Having in place a set of clear guidelines setting out how your communities can be used is helpful, as you have something you can refer and draw attention to quickly and easily. A clear set of internal protocols setting out how to respond to different types of breaches of your guidelines is also useful. But even in the most unreasonable situation you should also pay close attention to how you are seen to police your community, notably through the language and tone of your interventions. For example, blocking or banning people sometimes results in additional aggravation from the individuals concerned or even from the broader community if it is seen to be unjustified, so it is usually best to warn offenders before cutting off the taps. And it is essential that you sound polite and professional even in the most demanding situations, and never dismissive or rude.

9

The Rogue Employee

Like it or not, employees have always been able to hurt their employers. Confidential documents are exchanged for brown envelopes. An internal memo is leaked to a journalist, access to the deeper reaches of the company IT system is passed to a third party, someone conducts an unauthorized or illegal trade. Deliberate actions of this kind can be extremely damaging, raising serious questions about an organization's leadership, culture, and values. Fortunately, they have also been relatively rare.

No longer. Thanks to the social web, disgruntled staffers can now all too easily undermine or embarrass their employers. We saw earlier how Amy Cheong dragged her employer Singapore insurance firm NTUC Income into the spotlight with offensive comments about Malay weddings on her personal Facebook page. And how Hong Kong-based herbal jelly manufacturer Hoi Tin Tong was allegedly smeared by one of its own suppliers. Thankfully most issues involving employees on the social web are not triggered by the lone operator hell-bent on harming his employer but by people doing things that are thoughtless or silly or that may make management uncomfortable. The trouble with social media is that even the most banal error or thoughtless accusation can take off like wildfire.

Applebee's server abuses customer privacy

On January 25, 2013, Pastor Alois Bell took her congregation to her local Applebee's restaurant in St Louis after an evening service. At the end of the meal the pastor received her receipt, only to cross out the 18% gratuity and write "I give God 10% why do you get 18." Several days later another server at the restaurant took a photo of the receipt and, figuring other users would find it "entertaining" posted it to Reddit under the headline "My mistake sir, I'm sure Jesus will pay for my rent and groceries."[1] The post triggered heated discussion, mostly accusing the pastor of being unreasonable and, given her position, hypocritical. Some people also took issue with the firm sharing its customers' details. A few hours later *The Consumerist* blog picked up the story, causing it to go viral.

Alerted by a friend that her receipt was online Pastor Bell lodged a complaint with Applebee's, which set about finding out what had happened, conscious that its own and its customer's reputations were caught in the cross wires and that there was little that could be done to stop the receipt circulating. Discovering that the receipt had been posted by a member of its staff the firm fired the server who had posted it online.

Shortly afterwards Applebee's posted the following statement to its Facebook page:

Our Guests' personal information – including their meal check – is private, and neither Applebee's nor its franchisees have a right to share this information publicly. We value our Guests' trust above all else. Our franchisee has apologized to the Guest and has taken disciplinary action with the Team Member for violating their Guest's right to privacy.

Rather than calming matters the statement incited further anger, but now it was the restaurant chain that was largely on the receiving end, accused of having unfairly dismissed its worker and putting its customers ahead of its own people. Forced onto the defensive, Applebee's posted another statement explaining its decision in more detail and quoting its social media policy which stated its employees were not allowed to share photos, videos, and audio recordings featuring customers on social media without permission. A contravention of these rules, it stated, would be "subject to disciplinary action, up to and including termination of employment."[2]

But this only seemed to make matters even worse. Why? Because another receipt signed by a customer had been discovered on another Applebee's franchisee Facebook page, suggesting the chain was being inconsistent in how it applied its policy (even if Applebee's does not actually set employee or social media standards for its franchisees). Thousands of people were now commenting, the discussion veered from anger to outright vitriol, Facebook pages started appearing calling for the server to be reinstated and Redditors set up a new thread to find her a new job – and throughout bloggers and the media feasted on the meltdown.

The relevance of Applebee's experience for handling rogue employee incidents is not immediately apparent. Most obviously it underlines the need for terminations to be proportionate and reasonable and shows that company policies, including HR and social media, should be consistently applied. Applebee's social media policy clearly states that breaches of customer privacy are regarded as a sack-able offense, and it was within its operational and legal rights to fire the server. Whether her dismissal was reasonable in the circumstances is debatable – she set out to make fun of the customer but perhaps not to harm her. And it seems unlikely that she set out consciously to abuse the customer's privacy or to harm her employer. On the other hand, abusing a customer's privacy is bad practice but humiliating a customer, even if not intentional, is not acceptable, even if they are horrible to you and appear hypocritical. Whatever the rights or wrongs of its decision, Applebee's seemed to have been panicked into making a hasty decision when it might have taken more time to assess the reputational aspects of the situation.

Set out your position quickly, clearly, and in full

Usually awkward and frequently embarrassing, employee incidents lift the lid on companies in ways many other incidents do not and tend to attract bloggers and journalists like flies. With the online community on your back for answers, you need to make a substantive response as quickly as possible. Applebee's moved relatively quickly to address its customer's privacy breach publicly. But the receipt had already gone viral and it ended up botching its statement.

Like many other kinds of incidents, you may know little about a rogue employee until it hits you in the face. Which means you will probably have to issue a short, anodyne, public holding statement acknowledging the issue, while you work out what has gone wrong and how you're going to deal with it. When Greg Smith announced his intention to quit Goldman Sachs in an op-ed for the *New York Times*, the bank issued a short three-sentence statement stating it disagreed with his views. Later that day, it shared with journalists an internal memo from its CEO to its employees defending its practices and culture. (But Goldman had in fact been caught napping. The story had gone live on the paper's website at 3am, and by the time its doors had re-opened that morning Smith's experiences had gone global.)

To stop a story going viral, or at least to influence how people see it, it is important to try and respond to an issue where it first surfaces. Applebee's should have responded direct to the discussion on Reddit. Instead it responded a few hours later on Facebook, where discussions were starting to escalate. But the cat was already out of the bag. By contrast, Goldman Sachs focused its response to Greg Smith on the *New York Times* – aside from being one of the most influential news organizations in the world, it was also where Smith's allegations had first appeared. The bank also knew that the other media that counted – the *Wall Street Journal*, *Bloomberg*, *CNN* would initially take their cue from The Gray Lady.

With so many employee incidents now happening on the social web, many organizations now have little choice other than to respond first on Twitter, Facebook, or Yelp. But the social web presents its own challenges. It is difficult to say much in 140 characters, and whilst it is generally considered best practice to keep Facebook posts short and punchy, this means your position can easily be misconstrued or taken out of context. Applebee's made the mistake of issuing a short statement on social media that failed to address the question on many people's minds: whether the server had been fired. By not addressing this question, even unintentionally, it appeared secretive. Nor did it clarify or support its position for another few hours, and when it did so it released information in dribs and drabs, implying it was unsure what to say or was not being fully open.

Both Applebee's and Goldman Sachs were limited by the fact that neither had a corporate blog. A blog would have enabled them to support their respective cases vividly and in more depth, supporting their case with documents, images, or video in an easily accessible manner to which they could have linked from Facebook and elsewhere.

Step back and don't get into fights

Employee incidents often raise questions about sensitive issues and may involve having to take a decision about someone's future, both of which can lead to difficult and sometimes emotional feedback from members of your community. This increases the pressure on making the "right" decision and may mean you have to defend your decision publicly. An employee incident that is particularly confrontational or damaging and appears based on flimsy grounds may require an aggressive response. This can involve pointing out factual inaccuracies or forcefully rebutting misleading statements. Goldman Sachs undermined Greg Smith ahead of the publication of his book *Why I Left Goldman Sachs: A Wall Street Story* by revealing that he had not raised concerns about the culture of the firm or the conduct of his colleagues during his performance reviews.

Yet aggressive responses also have their dangers. Painting an employee as a rotten apple is a classic defense that can work well when the individual is a true rogue or lacks the desire, resources, or residual support to make his case credibly. But this well-worn strategy is wearing thin: not everyone can get into the *New York Times*, but the social web means any disgruntled employee or former employee can get their voice heard and, if they appear credible and have the ear of their colleagues and of the media, can make life distinctly uncomfortable for corporate bosses. We saw earlier how former Olympus CEO Michael Woodford successfully used the web and online video to shame his former bosses and appeal to rank-and-file employees to support his case.

On the whole it is advisable to step back in rogue employee situations, particularly when the facts are less than clear or if the online community turns against you. With inequality and the low levels of pay earned by servers and temporary staffers an increasingly mainstream – and political – issue in the US (and elsewhere), it is less than surprising that the public sided with the server, especially given the provocation of the pastor. With the tide of opinion turning against it, Applebee's might have benefitted from realizing that defending its decision was not a battle it was going to win and that it would have to take the abuse thrown at it, while knowing that it would likely soon die down.

Bear in mind that stepping back from the online fray is not necessarily the same thing as deserting. Make sure you continue to ensure people are not threatening your people, unduly harassing one another, talking wildly off topic, or using the incident to promote their own products on your official pages. But beware also that deleting profane or harassing posts (even if they are auto-deleted by Facebook) or blocking repeat offenders may also be seen as censorship in a high-pressure situation, leading to even more vitriol.

Keep your staff in the loop and be consistent about what you say

A long-held rule of communications says that you should assume everything said internally is going to be shared externally. Never is this principle truer than today. Internal "town hall" meetings can easily be recorded and shared with outsiders, and employees can anonymously express their support for a so-called rogue or take fire at management on company review sites like Glassdoor.

As mentioned above, all Goldman Sachs employees received a note defending the bank's practices and culture in Lloyd Blankfein's name the same day that Greg Smith's attack appeared in the *New York Times*. And several months later it pre-empted the publication of Smith's book by vigorously defending its culture and values in a memo to its people before circulating it to journalists and publishing it on its website.[3] In these tricky situations it is also important to remind employees of the need for a united voice and the need to observe social media protocols.

Making sure everyone is on the same page would have been a higher stakes game for Goldman Sachs, as its very raison d'être was being questioned. But it would also have been reasonably confident that the loyalty and professionalism of its staff, and the fact the most Goldman people are not allowed access to social media at work, would have reduced the risk of an embarrassing intervention. Companies like Applebee's that employ many short-term contract staff with little long-term loyalty to the brand have to work particularly hard to ensure what they say is credible and consistent.

Address yourself to the community

Almost as important as what is said online is how you say it. Official statements concerning employee incidents tend to be highly scripted. And with good reason: they almost invariably deal with sensitive issues of the kind their employers would rather not see the light of day. But tight messaging and bureaucratic language does not work on the social web, which demands a more human voice and a light touch. The initial response Applebee's posted to its Facebook page sounds rather stiff and bureaucratic, which contributed to its poor reception.

Applebee's could also have benefitted by addressing its various statements direct to the community or to the individuals involved. "Hello everyone," "Dear customers," or "@joesmith, thank you for your feedback" makes it clear whom you are addressing and makes people feel like they are important and are being listened to. In particularly difficult situations it can also be helpful to have someone authoritative talking for you. The statements Applebee's made to its Facebook page were also posted to its website under the name of its CEO. However posts to official Facebook pages can only be made in a company's name, so making it clear on Facebook that these were being made in the CEO's name may have helped convince people that the matter was being dealt with right at the top of the organization.

chapter 10

The Committed Activist

The fortunes of big pressure groups such as Greenpeace, Friends of the Earth and Amnesty International have been transformed by the internet and by social media, enabling them to recruit supporters and mobilize opinion on a scale and with a precision never previously possible. Once largely restricted to physical protests and email campaigns, they can now make life extremely awkward for organizations in their sights by drawing on an infinitely expanded toolbox of online hoaxes, spoofs, petitions, video, and hijacks. With companies under increasing pressure to associate themselves with public issues and most using digital channels to market their wares, the weak spots in the corporate armory have expanded enormously.

Knowing how best to handle a campaign waged against you by a campaign group is a difficult and sometimes thankless task. Activists usually only mount direct pressure campaigns when they believe other options have been exhausted and, when they are up and running there's little middle-ground for constructive engagement, not least on social media where the opportunity for in-depth discussion is limited. Their aim is to make your life as awkward as possible until you publicly confess your sins and repent.

Shell sidesteps Greenpeace online parody attack

On June 7, 2012, a YouTube user called "kstr3l" uploaded a video showing a private send-off at Seattle's Space Needle for two of Shell's Arctic rigs going awry when a spigot erupted oil over the guest of honor. The video was quickly picked up by bloggers and went viral, recording over 500,000 views in a matter of days. With bloggers running the story, the mainstream media got interested, leading to hundreds of articles.

Journalists covering the story then received an email in Shell's name threatening them not to run the story and directing them to http://arcticready.com, a website that appeared (and continues to do – it remains live at the time of writing) identical to an official Shell site, from the logo and navigation system, to the style of the images, to the links to official Twitter profiles and Facebook pages. Visitors could even create their own Shell-branded adverts using stock images of icebergs, penguins, and polar bears, with the most creative to be mounted on a billboard outside Shell's offices in Houston (Figure 10.1).

Over 12,000 ads were created, few of which were positive about the firm. And they kept coming for weeks. Of course, many quickly realized the campaign was a hoax but it seems a sizable minority did not, and their confusion was only made worse by

FIGURE 10.1 Mock Shell Let's Go advertisements

the appearance several weeks later of a Twitter account with the handle @ShellisPrepared under the name of Shell's Media team, the aim of which was to monitor and respond to "slanderous statements made toward Royal Dutch Shell."

We're working overtime to remove libelous ads.

This mess will be cleared up shortly. Stay tuned.

Our team is working overtime to remove inappropriate ads. Please stop sharing them.

The tweets also implied Shell's team had little idea what it was doing in social media.

Listen, it's my first day. I'm good with facebook but I don't understand why everyone can see my tweets.

PLEASE DO NOT RETWEET ANY OF OUR TWEETS. They are intended for their @ recipients only!

But they also went further, threatening legal action against anyone who mentioned the ads or retweeting others mentioning the Arctic Ready campaign.

WE'RE FLATTERED BY THE ATTENTION BUT PLEASE STOP! We'd hate to get the #Shell legal team involved.

Printed. 157 pieces of paper. Wasted a lot of trees but WORTH it. You guys are in trouble ...

I am about to print the list and take it to #Shell legal. You have five minutes to delete your tweets.

In fact, the entire campaign had been cooked up. The guest of honor at the private launch was an activist named Dorli Rainey who had infamously been pepper-sprayed by police during the Occupy Seattle movement the previous year, and the video, website, and social media profiles were all part of an elaborate hoax organized by Greenpeace and agitprop duo The Yes Men to highlight the oil firm's activities in the Arctic.

Shell's official response was limited to a brief statement posted to its Alaska website a few weeks after the fake video first appeared disclaiming any role in the campaign.[1] It did not intervene in any discussions, try to shut down site, or go after Greenpeace for infringing its trademarks. However the story had more or less run its course by the time Shell's response was published, and it received little attention.

What we can learn from how Shell handled Arctic Ready

Don't be provoked

Most activist campaigns have a single over-riding objective: to force change by making as many people as possible aware of your behavior and by encouraging them to act. But in a world in which we are constantly being called on to sign petitions against over-fishing or abuses of human rights or dig our hands into our pockets to support a friends' charity bike-ride, activists have to find increasingly unusual, ingenious, or compelling ways of cutting through the clutter and gaining our support.

Web-based parodies and hoaxes are a great way of doing this – they are cheap to make, easy to develop, and enable their backers to evaluate on the go how their message is getting across. They are also an established part of the activist toolkit for another important reason: they make it easy to use humor to attract attention and build interest in what are often emotive though complex issues. As the Poynter Institute has pointed out, Arctic Ready constituted "a new landmark in the history of hoaxes." Greenpeace developed an entire fake online ecosystem, mimicked attacks against itself, threatened legal action in Shell's name, and used Shell logos and other materials in a blatantly unauthorized way. All of which ensured that Greenpeace got acres of online buzz and media coverage. The Arctic Ready website drew over 2 million views in a matter of weeks.

But the campaign also had another objective: to provoke Shell into making a foolish or disproportionate response that could then be used against it. When your reputation is being mauled on Twitter and your boss is on your back imploring you to make it all go away, it is only too easy to rush your response. The oil firm could have tried to shut down the campaign on the basis that it infringed its intellectual property. Or it could have mounted a spirited public defense of its actions in the Arctic. But Shell realized that neither option was likely to do it many favors. Responding to Greenpeace's arguments would have meant getting into an online Mexican stand-off in which there would likely be no clear winners. Taking the activists to court would have meant providing Greenpeace with another platform from which they could make their case and which Shell was not guaranteed to win anyway as the campaign was not necessarily instantly recognizable as a spoof. So it opted for a low-key response that confirmed the campaign was false while trying to draw as little attention as possible to it.

Let them have their say

It is easy to be angered, upset, or scared by an activist attack. Activists jeopardize your hard work and profits, and much of what they demand appears to do little other than advance their own narrow agenda. But while you may not like or agree with what the activists are saying, it is important to realize that they are also entitled to have a point of view and, provided it is not deliberately false or misleading, their perspective is just as legitimate as your own and that is very likely going to be counter-productive to try to shut down the discussion or be seen to not take it seriously or mock it.

Sure, if your attackers are saying something that is demonstrably false then there is a strong case to rebut these claims directly and publicly or they can quickly become established facts. Shell publicly confirmed the Arctic Ready campaign was a hoax. But it took them several weeks to do so and arguably they should have moved more quickly if they were to stem the number of people who seemed to believe it was genuine. Equally if you have good reason to believe the public are largely behind you then there may be good reason to respond aggressively. One sound tactic is to get the most authoritative, trusted experts you can find to speak out in your favor. Ideally these should be independent voices, though you can also draw on your own people, as long as they are clearly identified as such.

But you should always remember that your detractors' views are just as valid as your own, however subjective they may be. Greenpeace may have been using underhand methods to gain attention but the underlying message of its campaign – that the fragile ecosystem of the Arctic was in danger – was legitimate, even if it threatened Shell's interests.

Play to the broader community

There's often little to be gained by responding directly to an activist attack. Negotiations will probably have run into a brick wall by this point and your detractors are left with the last substantive weapon left to them – applying public pressure in order to force you back to the negotiating table. They are unlikely to listen to what you've got to say online and any direct interaction is only going to be heated.

Rather you should be thinking of the broader community which, after all, is what you really need to be concerned about. There's little that's attractive about a big corporate Goliath seen to be trampling on a David, even if the David is from a well-funded group such as Greenpeace. So it is essential that you are seen as patient, polite, and considerate. Finding the right tone is critical.

In the face of severe provocation and public ridicule, Shell was commendably patient during Arctic Ready. Its public statement underlined this. Simple and to the point, it made clear that the oil firm had nothing to do with the campaign or the ads that were being produced in their name and noted that it had not filed any legal action on the matter. The tone was refreshingly informal and unbureaucratic. Yet there's arguably also a scintilla of condescension in its final words:

> ... in the spirit of intelligent debate on such a serious topic, we continue to offer our own (genuine) views as well as a few real facts about the challenges and opportunities of arctic exploration at http://shell.com/alaska

A final point – bear in mind that what you are seeing online may not be what it appears. The fact that hundreds or thousands of people may have "liked" a Facebook post or comment by your attackers does not necessarily translate into meaningful dislike or distrust of you. Rather it may indicate something that people find moderately interesting or are inclined to support passively but which they are not inclined to get behind in a truly active way.

Let the community come to your defense

Activists are only effective when they are seen as credible and are trusted. Like companies they spend years building their reputations. But like anyone's reputation, the reputations of activists can come undone in seconds, a risk made all the greater by the openness of social media. Greenpeace and The Yes Men took a calculated risk with the Arctic Ready campaign by pushing imitation to a legal and some would say ethical extreme. And not everyone was happy about it: feedback on YouTube to the video of the fake launch event and on Greenpeace's website to a blog post[2] by a former Greenpeace staffer giving the inside story of the campaign were met with roughly equal measures support and derision, with many people arguing that the campaign was deceptive, naïve, and damaged the campaign group's credibility. Others accused Greenpeace of being too obsessed with the media rather than driving actual change.

Occasionally the community will do your job for you. In early 2013, a well-known nationalist blog in Singapore attempted to boycott Philippine fast-food chain Jollibee's launch into the island on the basis that it "unlike other multi-national fastfood restaurants like McDonald's and KFC which hire mainly Singaporeans and even the disabled and elderly, Jollibee Singapore intends to hire their fellow pinoys to fill up jobs in their latest Singapore venture." But by closely analyzing exactly what Jollibee's recruitment materials had said on its website, Facebook page, and in its press release, local food blogger Daniel Ang was able to prove that these claims were disingenuous and taken out of context,[3] forcing the blog to backtrack and leading to a massive wave of online buzz and media coverage. Jollibee's launch far exceeded its expectations.

At other times you may need to arm your supporters. Shell's public statement encouraged people to visit its Arctic website to discover how it approaches exploration, safety, and manages its relationships with local communities and read about its approach to exploration. But few people would have seen the statement, as it was issued when the worst of the fuss had died down and was buried on a local website. Had it felt truly under threat, Shell could have publicized its activities far more strongly by working with sympathetic bloggers, developing videos to support its case, or even pulling people to its site by buying keywords on Google or Facebook.

Restore order when the heat dies down

Fighting fire with fire is a risky bet when it comes to activist attacks, as it is not only likely to antagonize your attackers but also increases the likelihood that the broader community may think you are using or abusing your corporate might to dampen or silence a legitimate debate. Above all, you need to be extremely careful about deleting comments on your official channels when the eyes of the world are on you, even ones that stray close to breaking your online community guidelines. Deleting or renaming false social media accounts mid-attack is also a dangerous game.

Nonetheless you can start to take firmer control of the situation online if and when the worst of the heat has cooled or the tide starts to turn to turn in your favor. You may already have been rebutting the most obviously misleading statements by sending people to your website or encouraging your supporters to counter all the negative views with some thoughts of their own. Now's the time to do this more firmly. This can also be a useful moment to address false social media accounts and other legal issues.

Shell waited some time to address the fake social media profiles lined up against it, and then it focused on removing the @ShellisPrepared Twitter profile on the basis that it clearly contravened Twitter's Impersonation Policy, a task in which it was successful. However other fake pages and profiles, notably the @ArcticReady Twitter profile and Shell Arctic Ready Facebook page, in addition to the ArcticReady.com website, were left standing. Why? Because while removing them may have proved possible from a legal point of view the uproar that is likely to have ensued was probably not worth the effort (and cost).

chapter 11

The Hostile Journalist

Dealing with journalists has always been a dicey business. You have little idea where they get their information from, are unsure about the nature of their agenda, and have little control over what the article they are writing is going to say. And then the facts of the article may be wrong, the context skewed, you are misquoted and, if you are lucky enough to get a public retraction, it is usually buried at the bottom of a page that few people read. And now you have to deal with web journalists and bloggers pumping stuff out as quickly as possible, unconcerned about the facts and with little interest in publishing corrections.

In this environment there's little point in endlessly trying to put the record straight – it easily appears petty and can strain valuable relationships. But this is not to say you don't have options. The social web may have tipped the balance of power away from big corporations to the man on the street and from traditional media to the digerati but it also enables you to set out your side of the story direct to your audiences and hold journalists and bloggers publicly to account. But you've got to be careful how you do this – social media is a two-edged sword that must be handled with real dexterity.

Tesla refutes *New York Times* 'fake' test drive

In January 2013, electric car manufacturer Tesla invited veteran *New York Times* journalist John M. Broder to test its two new Superchargers on the Interstate 95 between Washington and Boston with one of its acclaimed Model S electric cars. In the February 8 write-up of his experience in the Sunday edition of the paper, Broder praised described the Model S as "ultrahip" and a "technological wonder" but went on to describe how, in very cold weather and despite his efforts to reduce strain on the batteries by driving slowly, lowering the climate control, and multiple calls for support to Tesla officials, the car failed to live up to its mileage claim and did not make the distance between the two chargers, and ended shutting down on an exit ramp in Branford, Connecticut.[1] "If this is Tesla's vision of long-distance travel in America's future ... and the solution to what the company calls the 'road trip problem,' it needs some work," Broder observed acidly.

Four days later billionaire entrepreneur and Tesla CEO Elon Musk took to Twitter to rip into Broder and the *NY Times*, setting off several days of controversy:

> NYTimes article about Tesla range in cold is fake. Vehicle logs tell true story that he didn't actually charge to max & took a long detour.

Which he followed up with:

> Tesla blog coming soon detailing what actually happened on Broder's NYTimes 'range test'. Also lining up other journalists to do same drive.

Tesla data logging is only turned on with explicit approval of Tesla customers but after Top Gear BS, we always keep it on for media.

Btw, more free East Coast Superchargers coming soon. Will allow lower initial charge, v high speed trip and long detours, like NYTimes drive.

A serial entrepreneur at the helm of one of the most innovative and talked about firms in the world, Musk would have been pretty certain that a direct assault on the integrity of one the *NY Times'* top journalists would attract attention. And so it proved: thousands of people passionately defended both the car manufacturer and the publisher online, the news media smelled a story, and Musk was invited onto *CNBC* to make his case.

Not to be outdone, Broder preempted Musk's blog post by defending his article on the paper's *Wheels* blog, saying he'd be willing to do another test drive when the additional Superchargers had come online.[2] The following day, Musk posted a detailed rebuttal of Broder's original review on Tesla's corporate blog, arguing it did "not factually represent Tesla technology, which is designed and tested to operate well in both hot and cold climates" and that it "simply did not accurately capture what happened and worked very hard to force our car to stop running." Broder, Musk claimed, had failed to listen to the advice of Tesla officials when he phoned expressing his concerns about the car's range and, according to the vehicle logs, which he also published online, the car's battery had never run out of energy, and he had not recharged the car to the extent he had claimed.[3] "Our request of the New York Times is simple and fair," he wrote, "please investigate this article and determine the truth."

The following day Broder hit back on the paper's *Wheels* blog with a point-by-point rebuttal of a number of Musk's points, including that the car battery had never run out of energy and that he had ignored the advice of Tesla officials. He ended by asserting that the Tesla CEO had personally apologized to him and admitted the "charging stations should be closer together."[4] Meantime *NY Times* Public Editor Margaret Sullivan confirmed on the paper's *Public Editor's Journal* blog that she was trying to get to the bottom of the story and would report back when she had been able to draw her conclusions.[5] Four days later she returned to defend Broder's integrity ("I do not believe Mr Broder hoped the drive would end badly. I am convinced he took on the test drive in good faith, and told the story as he experienced it") but went on to say that she believed he failed to use good judgment when driving the car and took "casual and imprecise notes."[6]

Musk later admitted on Bloomberg TV the spat had led to "hundreds of cancelled orders" and had hit Tesla's valuation by tens of thousands and perhaps USD 100 million.[7] However the episode did not stop the firm going on to report its best ever results for Q1 2013.

Move quickly

A researcher at San Diego's Supercomputer Center recently estimated that the average internet user in the US will spend 15.5 hours a day watching TV, surfing the web, and on their smartphones in 2015, in the process consuming the equivalent of nine DVDs worth of news, entertainment, and information.[8] In this overwhelming media smorgasbord, attention spans have shriveled and the so-called 24-hour news cycle has become a thing of the past, replaced by a torrent of mini-cycles driven by Twitter, video, and Google news rankings. So you have to move extremely fast to catch people's attention before the wave recedes, perhaps never to reappear.

Tesla took four days to respond, which is too slow these days. However in this instance Musk could afford the risk of the news cycle ebbing as he knew he could rely on his name alone to get it flowing again. That said, Tesla knew Broder's article was going to be negative and even if it did not know the precise nature of the complaints it could and arguably should have been in a position to respond more or less immediately. The fact that it wasn't created the impression that it was either unprepared, unsure of its facts, or had something to hide.

Pick your Turf carefully and tread sensitively

Most PR professionals will tell you that if they responded to every false rumor, inaccuracy, or mistake created by journalists, not to say bloggers and tweeting customers, they would have almost no time for anything else. But time is not the only constraint – it is also true that correcting every misplaced dot and comma and rebutting every tall story out there won't win you many friends amongst those on the receiving end and can end up doing as much harm as good. That said, some media outlets, journalists, and bloggers are more influential than others, and if they make a bad error or serious allegation about you then you should strongly consider setting the record straight. But be aware that taking on a publication as high profile and esteemed as the *NY Times* is also a high stakes gamble and you need to be absolutely confident of your facts.

You should also be careful of going in all guns blazing and making it appear some kind of grudge match. Accusing Broder on Twitter of a lack of integrity was only going to infuriate the journalist and alienate his editors and it almost certainly provoked Broder to pre-empt Musk's blog post with his own retort. Musk would have been better advised to have stuck to the facts and pitched his case in a constructive tone that made it easier for the *NY Times* to accept it may have gotten some of its facts wrong and that appealed to the better instincts of his customers, potential customers, and the general public. He might also have given the journalist a chance to defend himself privately in the first instance and, if a clarification or retraction was still not forthcoming, then to have taken it to his editor. A public attack on an organ like the *NY Times* should be your last line of defense, not your first.

Tell your story persuasively

Most important of all, you need to make your case as compellingly as you possibly can, using photographs, charts, data, and bullet points to explain your position and provide context and proof. And here's where social media and in particular the corporate blog excel, as they enable you to tell your story in full Technicolor on a channel you own and can control and update in real-time as things develop. Having used its blog before to rebut media reviews and news stories (notably the 2008 BBC *Top Gear* review mentioned by Musk in his tweets that ended with Jeremy Clarkson saying its Roadster model "absolutely doesn't work" – a review that went to court on grounds of defamation but which Tesla lost a month after its run-in with the *New York Times*), Tesla had a feel for how to use these channels in its defense, down to providing the vehicle logs that gave its case real substance. As Margaret Sullivan noted, "A little red notebook in the front seat is no match for digitally recorded driving logs, which Mr. Musk has used, in the most damaging (and sometimes quite misleading) ways possible, as he defended his vehicle's reputation."

The only problem with this kind of approach is that even the most cogent and factual response may be ignored by the offending publication and, more important, by the audiences to whom you are making your case. Sometimes it takes doing something unusual, provocative, or humorous to get attention. After two Princeton researchers applied a mathematical model used for disease control to predict levels of engagement on Facebook would evaporate and that the social network would lose 80% of its peak user base between 2015 and 2017,[9] a data scientist at Facebook responded by publishing a brilliant and humorous riposte on its own blog that used the number of page likes on Facebook and volume of searches on Google as a basis for predicting that "Princeton may be in danger of disappearing entirely."[10]

In a similar vein, Walmart responded to a June 2014 *New York Times* op-ed on inequality in the US by opinion contributor Timothy Egan that stated the retailer was "a big part of the problem" whose "humiliating wages force thousands of employees to look to food stamps"[11] by publishing a marked-up version of the original article to its own blog that highlighted what it saw as inaccurate statements and unfair allegations, suggested stronger sources, and corrected iffy grammar.[12] In itself this kind of approach might not ordinarily have caused much interest but in this case the company was sufficiently high profile, the topic noteworthy, and the retort conclusive and humorous, giving it a good chance that it would be picked up by other news media and talked about online (Figure 11.1).

Activate your supporters

It's all very well concocting a strong, witty, or distinctive defense, but that in itself is no guarantee that anyone is going to notice it. So you'll also need to think about who you want to see it and how you're going to get it to them. Walmart included a link to its blog post in its weekly email to journalists. Tesla promoted its blog posts vigorously through its official Twitter and Facebook channels; it also encouraged other news organizations to do the same test drive and to report their findings. And several of its customers went out in freezing weather to test the route themselves, recording and posting their efforts online.

Sometimes you may want to go further. After a June 2011 *New York Times* article on gas industry fracking had singled out

Tim—
Thanks for sharing your first draft. Below are
a few thoughts to ensure something inaccurate
doesn't get published.

Hope this helps.
—WMT

The Corporate Daddy

Walmart, Starbucks, and the Fight Against Inequality

JUNE 19, 2014

Timothy Egan

For some time now, Republicans in Congress have given up the pretense of doing anything to improve the lot of most Americans. Raising the minimum wage? They won't even allow a vote to happen. Cleaner air for all? They may partially shut down the government in a coming fight on behalf of major polluters. Add to that the continuing obstruction of student loan relief efforts, and numerous attempts to defund health care, and you have a party actively working to make life miserable for millions.

Yay!

So, our nation turns to Starbucks. And Walmart. In the present moment, both of those global corporate monoliths are poised to do more to affect the huge chasm between the rich and everybody else than anything that's likely to come out of John Boehner's House of Representatives.

As long as the Supreme Court says that corporations are citizens, they may as well act like them. Starbucks is trying to be dutiful — in its own prickly, often self-righteous, spin-heavy way — while Walmart is a net drain on taxpayers, forcing employees into public assistance with its poverty-wage structure.

We are the largest tax payer in America. Can we see your math?

"In the last few years, we have seen the fracturing of the American dream," said the Starbucks chief executive, Howard Schultz, in announcing a company plan to reimburse the cost of college tuition for employees. "The question for all of us is, should we accept that, or should we try to do something about it?"

We see more associates move off of public assistance as a result of their job at Walmart. Here is one story: http://bit.ly/1m34poq

FIGURE 11.1   Excerpt from Walmart annotated response to *New York Times* article on inequality

US-based oil and gas firm Chesapeake Energy as overstating its productivity and profits – one of a series of skeptical pieces the paper had run on fracking – then Chesapeake CEO Aubrey McClendon circulated a detailed three-page rebuttal to his employees and encouraged them to share it externally. Chesapeake spokesman E. Blake Jackson actively responded to mentions of the article and to the topic of fracking through the company's official Twitter profile, shared positive articles in the mainstream media, and retweeted people supporting his firm.

Unusually, the firm also bought a series of Promoted Tweets for terms such as #naturalgas and @nytimes, all of which linked back to its Facebook page, to which McClendon's email had also been posted. This is where social media beats traditional ways of managing negative incidents hands down. Think about it: until recently the only way to respond to a negative article or review was through the letters page of the newspaper, an appeal to the editor or perhaps the publisher, or, if things got really bad, by forking out for an advert. Twitter and Facebook enable you to promote your message to a large and influential audience of bloggers, journalists, and industry experts and to drive action and discussion by providing a clear call to action/link. And you can do so in an incredibly focused way, targeting people by interest as well as by location, demographics, and behavior, or combinations thereof.

chapter 12

The Backfiring Campaign

Just as the social web is a powerful opportunity for marketers and communicators to reach and persuade people of the merits of their products and services, it can also be a double-edged sword that results in your carefully crafted efforts being sliced apart in full public view. Of course, some campaigns set out to cause controversy; a thick skin goes with the territory. Benetton's 2011 online Unhate ad campaign promoting "a culture of tolerance" and intended to "combat hatred around the world" featuring the Pope kissing an Egyptian imam may have scooped the Grand Prix at the Cannes advertising festival but it also resulted in an uproar amongst religious groups, condemnation by the Vatican and White House, and led to the image being withdrawn. [1] But it had achieved what it set out do: generate press coverage and digital ink.

In most cases, however, a campaign will backfire unexpectedly as a result of it being seen as inappropriate, badly managed, or poorly timed. Suddenly you find a swarm of people mocking or chastising you on Twitter and on your Facebook page and you face the tricky decision of what to do. How you choose to respond will depend on many factors, including the public mood and your appetite for damage.

ING Direct Canada suffers mental health backlash

Personal finances are a personal, knotty, and frequently emotional topic for many people. If anxieties about whether we are saving enough for our kids' education and retirement aren't enough, widespread stories of mis-sales and poor performance, made worse by the global financial crisis, have deepened mistrust in banks and financial advisors.

Against this background the Canadian arm of personal bank ING Direct (since rebranded as Tangerine) launched a multi-channel campaign in January 2013 to promote its Retirement Savings Plan (RSP) and Tax-Free Savings Accounts (TFSAs), likening the process of choosing a bank to a sickness leading to stress and sleeplessness. The Are You Suffering? campaign centered on a TV spot showing a depressed man with "RSP" unable to eat or sleep, who is cured by a visit to the bank,[2] and was to be buttressed by a series of online ads showing people how to self-diagnose the fake illness alongside a makeover of five of the bank's café's into "financial pharmacies." We touched on the campaign in Chapter 5.

Initially feedback to the campaign was muted, but within two days the bank and its CEO Peter Aceto started to receive emails and posts to their Facebook pages and on Twitter complaining that the advert was disrespectful to people with mental health issues. The CEO of the Canadian Mental Health Association chimed in online arguing that almost one in five Canadians suffered some form of mental illness.

@CEO_INGDIRECT As a person with a chronic disease I find your RSP commercial totally inappropriate. It is in total bad taste. Thank you.

> ING Direct 'Suffering from RSP' commercial in exception-
> ally poor taste. Mocking mental illness, very clever.
>
> @ingdirect your newest commercial is despicable. Until
> you remove it from circulation, I'll be sending a lot of info
> your way.

Realizing that the campaign was touching a raw nerve, the bank pulled the campaign in its entirety and posted a message to Facebook (and an abbreviated version of its Facebook response to Twitter).

> We'd like to thank all our Clients and followers for their
> feedback. Whilst it was never our intention to make light
> of any health concerns related to mental illness, we have
> heard you loud and clear. We have decided to remove our
> RSP commercial from TV. It may take a few days for it to
> come off air, but the process is in motion. Please accept
> our apologies if you were offended by our commercial.

Reaction to ING's move was positive, with people thanking it for doing the right thing and moving so quickly. But what should we learn from its U-turn from a social media perspective?

Be sensitive but don't overreact

Oftentimes the first negative reaction you'll hear to a marketing campaign is through the social web. Often initially arriving in dribs and drabs, some of the feedback may be excoriating but it may also reflect a wide spectrum of opinion, making it difficult to know if the minority is justified and how mainstream its views are. In fact, a test of ING's Suffering campaign ahead of launch had not revealed anything negative. So it was understandable that the bank waited a couple of days while it figured out whether continuing to run it would lead to significant, long-term damage to its business and reputation or whether the gathering clouds were in fact little more than a storm in a teacup. But the feedback started accelerating and some was highly emotional, including an email Peter Aceto received from a man whose son, who he did not know suffered from depression, had committed suicide at university. At this point Aceto decided to re-watch the ads and, realizing they could easily be seen in another light, went back to the online community and acknowledged he had heard the feedback and was considering it thoroughly. Within 24 hours of receiving the suicide email he had withdrawn the campaign, replacing it with re-purposed older adverts.

Despite the negative opinion being in a minority, ING was seen to do the right thing and quickly won back the trust of its audiences. But sometimes the tea leaves are less easy to read. In November 2012, Asda supermarket ran an advertising campaign in the UK that showed a young mother struggling to cope with all the Christmas preparations while the rest of her family did nothing. "Behind every great Christmas there's mum," the spot chimed. Immediately the retailer started to be accused of sexism - online, through its advertising regulators, and in the mainstream media. But it also received thousands of likes on its Facebook page, positive feedback on Twitter, and support by prominent journalists and commentators who felt it was being unfairly slammed. Rather than pulling the campaign, Asda decided to keep it going while issuing a statement apologizing for the upset it had caused and clarifying that it was not its intention to offend anyone and that it respected all parents.

To their credit, rather than rushing into a decision, both firms managed to keep cool heads in awkward and confusing situations involving highly emotive topics and came out only a little worse for wear. Asda, appreciating the deep divergence of views about its advert, figured it could soldier on, a decision that proved largely warranted. It is likely that ING Direct also made the right call, if for different reasons. A relatively new brand in a highly competitive industry beset by trust issues, it figured the short-term commercial costs were worth sacrificing for the health of its reputation in the longer term.

Much, of course, depends on the local context and culture. Also worth bearing in mind is that ING Direct was in a better position than many firms to gauge the public mood as its CEO was a social media enthusiast known for publishing his views online and for personally answering questions from customers and others. Instinctively he has a good feel for online issues. However, most organizations do not have the luxury of having a CEO with his ear so firmly to the ground. In the absence of any critical mainstream media coverage or complaints to regulators, you will need to find ways of bringing alive the urgency of the situation and the broader context while spelling out the different options in a balanced, professional manner.

Admit the error of your ways

We all make mistakes. We can be naïve, greedy, or too fixated on the end goal to see what we are really walking into. And people are largely accepting of our misdemeanors, provided we learn the lessons and don't repeat them. But to suggest you have learned from past experiences requires us to admit we have strayed in the first place, and there is little that irritates people more than when we are unable to accept we've done something wrong.

ING Direct may not have intended to make light of mental illness but it also realized that it could and should have seen the broader picture and that its actions were causing real discomfort, not to say outrage among some people. So it had little to lose and much to gain by confessing it had screwed up while confirming its intentions had been noble. Asda, on the other hand, had not messed up to the same degree (even if the noise had been louder) and therefore had less need to state it had erred.

How we admit our wrongdoing is also important. ING Direct was dealing with an issue that was playing out largely in social media. A marketing industry publication had covered the launch of the campaign but the financial and business media had not yet covered it. Accordingly the bank decided to respond primarily through its official Facebook and Twitter accounts, and CEO Peter Aceto also fessed up on his own social media accounts. Conversely, with the mainstream media on its backs, a much greater proportion of Asda's response was made through conventional media outreach.

Repent sincerely

The immediacy and connectedness of the internet means it is important that you think as carefully about the tone of what you say as the message and timing. Eating humble pie is never easy, especially in public, but you need to remember that the social web does not provide you the same comfort of a barrier between yourselves and the world at large as a newspaper or even a TV interview. You should also bear in mind that social media users have a built-in nose and intolerance for anything that is seen as insincere.

You can go a long way to establishing the appropriate tone by being seen to be aware of the situation, listening to all points of view, and admitting that you've made an error. But it is also about your language and tone of voice, which should be friendly, humble, and direct, conspicuously avoiding weasel-wording and jargon, which only gives the impression that you are trying to avoid the issue or cover something up. While an example of a program rather than a campaign backfiring, the way General Mills chose to back out of the controversial update to its legal terms described in Chapter 1 is instructive. Here's how the U-turn was communicated on the firm's corporate blog:[3]

As has been widely reported, General Mills recently posted a revised set of Legal Terms on our websites. Those terms – and our intentions – were widely misread, causing concern amongst our customers.

So we've listened – and we're changing them back to what they were before.

The reaction to the statement was savage, with much of the ire focused on the second sentence, which implied the problem rested with its customers rather than the company itself. Whatever language and tone of voice you choose, it needs to be in line with your company's values. J.P. Morgan backed out of the question and answer session with its vice chairman it had arranged on Twitter under the hashtag #AskJPM with a brief, elegant, if somewhat terse tweet admitting its mistake.

Tomorrow's Q&A is cancelled. Bad Idea. Back to the drawing board.

One thing to note in the context of managing backfires: humor can help defuse a situation but must be used carefully and not indicate you don't care about your customers. Qantas acknowledged that its Luxury campaign was melting down with a tweet published about two hours into the promotion, followed by another spelling the end of the campaign.

Wow some very creative tweeps out there. Keep the entries coming #QantasWeHearYou

At this rate our #QantasLuxury campaign is going to take years to judge

The airline's approach plays nicely to Australians' deadpan, ironic sense of humor but is unlikely to have worked in the US nor for J.P. Morgan. And a humorous exit wouldn't go down well anywhere if you've crossed a boundary as sensitive as mental illness or sexism. ING Direct and Asda conspicuously avoided humor.

It can also pay real dividends to apologize, as long as it is warranted and done appropriately. Campaigns that break cultural norms or are seen to deal with sensitive societal issues such as mental illness or sexism will usually merit an apology. But in many cases an apology is not needed; admitting the mistake and promising to do better is sufficient. But neither will get the online community off your back if it is seen as insincere.

There's also the question of who should do the apologizing. Both ING Direct and Asda successfully got across that they were sorry for the anguish they had caused. But the bank's statement came across strongest when it was articulated by Peter Aceto, even if the words he used were more or less identical to what the company as a whole was saying. Partly this was because they came from the CEO himself and were therefore seen as more credible, and partly as he said it in a less formal way:

Never intended to make light of mental illness w. our RRSP TV ads. Please accept our apologies if U were offended. Spots 2B removed.

In addition to posting statements to its social media profiles, ING Bank also made a big effort to respond direct to anyone who had commented negatively on the issue online – a nice personal touch that indicated that they really cared about their customers.

* * *

Rogue employees, activist customers, and backfiring campaigns are happening with increasing frequency. While they can be sharp and ugly, if handled appropriately most are over relatively quickly and the impact is muted. But there are also the kinds of problems that send an organization into a tailspin – an Exxon Valdez, Sony Pictures hack, or the collapse of the Rana Plaza garment factory in Bangladesh – bone fide crises in which senior management are diverted from their day-to-day responsibilities for days and sometimes weeks at a time.

How you handle a real crisis can mean the difference between life and death and determine how you are seen for long afterwards. While Malaysia Airlines has had to be taken private in the aftermath of its MH370 and MH17 disasters, Air Asia survived a series of incidents, including QZ8501 crashing into the Java Sea off Indonesia. Structural issues certainly played a big part in the demise of Malaysia Airlines but poor handling of the disappearance of MH370 and excellent communications by Air Asia CEO Tony Fernandes also contributed to one firm making it while the other went down. The next part of the book looks at how the social web can be used in a major crisis.

part III

Handling Crises

Headline Crime

chapter 13

The Changing Face of Crises

Every now and again something will go very badly wrong – one of your planes disappears, your factory catches fire, foreign ingredients are discovered in one of your best-known products. Unlike many of the incidents we saw in Part II, problems of this magnitude can paralyze senior leadership and severely impact the inner workings of your organization. They may also draw the attention of regulators and politicians, each with the power to put you out of business.

Having TV crews camped outside one's offices baying for blood is not an experience many of us would willingly go through, but at least you can control whether or not you're going to open the front door to make a statement and if you're going to take questions. By contrast the volatile, the two-way nature of the social web together with the potential for news and rumors to spread like wildfire makes it much more difficult to manage perceptions and makes it more even important that audiences are handled with confidence and sensitivity during high profile negative situations.

Crisis experts will always tell you that there is no silver bullet for handling crises as no one situation is the same. There is much truth in this and the social web has only made matters more convoluted. However there are still some basic lessons that can be learned from how crises are playing out today. In this final part of the book we will explore some overarching principles for how you can prepare for, respond to, and recover from crises using social media. First, however, it is useful to explore some ways the social web is changing the nature of crises.

More short, sharp shocks

With the exception of unexpected natural disasters such as the 2004 Indian Ocean tsunami, a data breach of the scale experienced by Sony Pictures in 2014 and other "unknown unknowns," the great majority of serious threats should (in theory) be understood, prepared for, and, when they hit, handled in a way that minimizes the damage. Research by the Institute of Crisis Management shows that little more than a decade ago the great majority of crises were attributable to "smoldering" issues such as internal strategic and corporate governance failures and external factors such as major political and regulatory change.[1]

Left to fester, these slow-burn issues eventually seep into the public domain and escalate into full-scale crises. For example, the official commission into BP's 2010 Gulf of Mexico spill found decisions by the oil company and its partners to cut costs and save time led to "systemic" failures that "might well recur."[2] Similarly Bank of America had almost certainly known that the introduction of its USD 5 debit card fee in 2011 was going to be unpopular yet it significantly underestimated the depth of anger felt towards it as an organization, a mistake that culminated in the loss of tens of thousands of its retail customers (as described in Chapter 4).

Fortunately the adoption of sophisticated and comprehensive approaches to managing risks and engaging stakeholders has helped keep the lid on many major corporate fires. But there has also been a parallel increase in the number of problems concerning day-to-day customer service, employee behavior, marketing, and other activities of the sort we have seen throughout this book. Poorly handled, these can quickly escalate into high-profile public incidents and even full-blown crises that bring the whole firm into disrepute (Table 13.1).

As we saw in Part II, it is not easy stopping a small-scale problem taking off online and becoming a major public story. Yet very few of these problems become bone fide crises; the volume of bad news that travels our way on a daily basis combined with the fact that our attention spans have become so short mean most of these stories disappear almost as fast they appear.

TABLE 13.1   Different types of negative situations

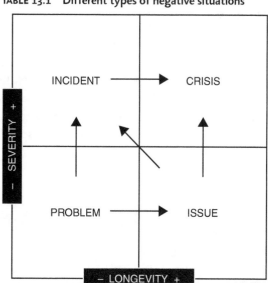

Source: Charlie Pownall.

Bad news travels faster, further, and stays longer

Whether a crisis is sudden or smoldering, news today moves at breakneck speed. And it will probably not just travel fast but also extraordinarily far in a very short space of time. On January 6, 2012, Korean-American Minhee Cho placed an order at Papa John's in Manhattan, New York, only to notice that her receipt described her as "lady chinky eyes." Offended, she placed a photo of the receipt on Twitter which quickly attracted hundreds of retweets and over 200,000 views. Picked up initially by a local newspaper, the story was then run on CNN and spread worldwide, gaining particular notoriety in South Korea, where the pizza outlet's local operation was forced to apologize to local customers.

Ms Cho's experience is backed by a 2013 study by law firm Freshfields Bruckhaus Deringer amongst 102 senior crisis communications professionals at multinationals in the UK and mainland Europe that found that a quarter of crises are picked up by the international media within one hour of an incident happening, and two-thirds within 24 hours.[3] The study also found that information also stays in the public eye for longer. Over half (53%) of crises were still in the news a month later, with social media reported to having had a "significant" impact on how the story spread in one half of cases. In addition, search engines index and display information and commentary about a crisis years later.

SOCIAL MEDIA DOESN'T MEAN ALL CRISES ARE GLOBAL

Crises may move further faster today but it is also important not to over-estimate their reach. Freshfields Bruckhaus Deringer observed in its research study that many crises spread to multiple markets more or less instantly. Yet there are plenty of scenarios when a crisis will remain local:

- **Footprint.** If an organization has no foreign operations, stakeholders, or relevance and where its reputation is local or national.
- **Language.** Where the language in which the company operates is little spoken outside its domestic borders, such as Japan.
- **Affinity.** Where potential for word of mouth is limited due to local, small-scale, or weak online affinity communities.

A case in point is Hoi Tin Tong, the Hong Kong-based herbal medicine manufacturer and retailer we met earlier that was hauled into the spotlight by a video alleging to show moldy jelly at one of its plants. Covered in detail by the local press, including the influential *South China Morning Post*, and the subject of considerable speculation in Hong Kong's hyper active online communities, the story proved immensely damaging to its operations in Hong Kong. Yet the story failed to catch light in mainland China and Macau, despite the firm's physical presence in southern China and the former Portuguese colony. Why? Perhaps because the firm is principally a local Hong Kong player and media coverage and online discussions were primarily in Cantonese, a language alien to most mainland Chinese.

Needless to say the speed at which information now travels means you now have minutes rather than hours to get across your side of the story, a tricky proposition when rumors are starting to spread on Twitter and you have little idea of what's really happening.

Openness is expected the moment a crisis starts

In addition to moving fast, one of the major challenges of the social web when you're faced with a crisis is that people expect you to be open, honest, and objective the instant something bad happens, something that doesn't come naturally to many people. Yet, as we saw in Part II of this book, the speed information moves and the intensity of discussions means saying nothing during the initial stages of an incident or crisis only gives the impression that you are being defensive and have something to hide. It also leaves you even more open to online rumors and conjecture.

In addition to providing timely, factual updates, today's culture of instant accountability means you are also expected to be publicly visible and responsive. Traditionally, interaction with outsiders during a crisis could be limited to carefully prepared scripts read out at stage-managed press conferences, community meetings, and employee town halls. But Facebook and other social platforms mean you are now in direct contact with the general public and expected to get actively involved in open, public discussions. This is not easy: many organizations find responding to awkward questions online hard enough at the best of times, let alone during a crisis. How, they ask, do you control the narrative when you don't have the facts and when everyone seems to have an opinion? How do you stay "on message" when social media requires an "authentic" human voice that doesn't keep bridging back to a set of prescribed key messages?

Smoking guns are harder to conceal

Under pressure as publicity about the Watergate break-in and bugging grew, President Richard Nixon deployed a variety of well-established techniques to thwart investigators and protect his public image, including concealing evidence, stopping people from connecting dots, shifting the blame onto others, and attempting to reframe the discussion into one about political survival and national self-interest. But with everything now in digital format and instantly recordable and sharable amongst large numbers of people connected by similar views and interests, it is now much easier to get at the truth and far harder to bury it.

In Chapter 1 we saw how Chinese authorities tried to bury (literally) two rail carriages after a collision involving one of its brand new high-speed trains outside the south-eastern city of Wenzhou killed 40 people, a maneuver quickly undone by skeptical locals with smartphones. Furthermore attempts by the authorities to muzzle media coverage through a series of directives instructing journalists to focus on the rescue efforts rather than investigate the cause of the incident and only to follow statements from "authoritative departments" were widely leaked.[4] The subsequent outcry forced Beijing into conducting an official inquiry, which found the problem to be the result of a combination of faulty designs, bidding irregularities, poor safety checks, and inadequate management oversight. The Wenzhou incident has been described as the moment social media was first successfully used to hold Beijing publicly accountable for a major incident.

Rumors and misinformation spread like wildfire

Crises are complex situations where the truth can be difficult to ascertain, especially in the early stages when everyone is talking but the facts remain unclear. During Watergate the facts were deliberately withheld, thereby ensuring that rumors and speculation dominated how people saw events from the moment the break-in was discovered to Nixon's final days in office, making it extremely difficult for Nixon's staff to control the narrative.

Yet it is safe to assume that had Twitter been invented in the 1970s, life would have been even trickier for Nixon. Social media has ensured rumor-mongering is no longer the preserve of political operatives and the chattering classes, but a sport played and consumed by amateurs and professionals alike. And the stakes can be high. During Hurricane Sandy's assault on New York in late October 2012, CNN ran a story revealing that the New York Stock Exchange was under three feet of water, only to discover it was a hoax concocted by hedge fund manager and political campaigner Shashank Tripathi under his popular Twitter pseudonym @comfortablysmug. There was also a rumor that all power in Manhattan was being shut down, which turned out to be another hoax by the same individual.

While not all rumors are deliberately misleading, even scares based on mistakes can cause havoc. One persistent rumor during Hurricane Sandy concerned a serious fire at Coney Island Hospital, yet this was later found to have originated from an update on a police scanner which police and firefighters use to trade and assess tips based on 911 calls, which are then investigated in person. In this case the tip in question was inaccurate but had quickly gone viral on Twitter. And while many of the updates, photographs, and videos shared on Twitter and Facebook by eyewitnesses to natural disasters and terrorist bombings are well-intentioned and a good deal of them useful, their sheer volume and the fact that it is difficult to establish the credibility of their sources usually results in additional public panic and further confuses the situation for police and emergency response teams.

Social data provides real-time insight

The cards can appear dauntingly stacked against you with rumors, conjecture, and hard news simultaneously running riot on Twitter. However the social web also enables you to quickly correct mis- and disinformation and communicate your side of the story direct with your audiences rather than through journalists and other intermediaries. Help is on hand in the form of a wealth of data that can help you listen for what's being said online about you, gauge the public mood, develop the appropriate response and assess its impact.

A study by China-based social business intelligence firm CIC and Ogilvy Public Relations on the impact of online buzz on 20 crises affecting foreign and local companies in China during 2013 discovered that purchase intent collapsed between an average 169 and 221% immediately the crisis was discovered, dropping to its lowest level four days after the incident.[5] The study goes on to analyze the impact of three different first responses – denial, admission and investigation. Unsurprisingly, an immediate and outright denial has the most negative impact on purchase intent, which collapses by over 400% on day one and changes little over the following week, while the immediate announcement of an investigation into the incident almost halves the decline in purchase intent on day one and does so again a week later. Interestingly, the study also discovered that launching an investigation is more effective than admitting the problem from the get-go and apologizing (Table 13.2).

The study also finds that admitting a problem exists and apologizing for it while failing to launch an investigation is almost as

TABLE 13.2   Impact of different crisis responses on purchase intent

Response	Change in purchase intention (%)		
	By day 1	By day 4	By day 7
Deny issue	–403%	–370%	–312%
Admit problem & apologize	–348%	–301%	–234%
Announce investigation	–219%	–156%	–113%

Source: Ogilvy Public Relations, CIC – 2014.

damaging as an outright denial, while a denial followed by an apology – whether forced or otherwise – causes the most damage of all.

* * *

The social web has changed the dynamics of crises in many ways. But while some of the tools and techniques used to track, mitigate, and respond to online threats are different to those used in offline crisis communications, many of the overarching principles remain the same. The findings of CIC and Ogilvy PR's China crisis study will relieve "traditional" crisis experts as they show the most effective online crisis responses are consistent with offline practices; which makes the business of preparing for crises playing out in social media – the subject of the next chapter – considerably simpler than reinventing the wheel.

chapter 14

Preparing for a Crisis

You could be forgiven for not knowing about Fonterra. After all, the company was only formed in 2001, the result of a merger of three of New Zealand's biggest dairy co-operatives. A private entity, it is also New Zealand's biggest business and the world's largest dairy trader, accounting for around 30% of the world's milk, butter, and cheese exports.

While you may not have heard of Fonterra itself you may know its products, which include Anchor butter, Anlene milk powder, and Tip Top ice cream. Household names in New Zealand and Australia, these and other brands are being aggressively marketed and sold in over 100 countries. In fact, many of its brands are also new; Fonterra was traditionally built on supplying dairy ingredients for others to manufacture and market. While this remains an important pillar of its business, the firm is now well along the path of transforming itself into a consumer-focused firm. Like many companies undertaking a similar journey, Fonterra has started to market its name and identity as a badge of quality.

Not that it has been all plain sailing. Fonterra has been accused of destroying tropical rainforests in Indonesia and Malaysia and polluting rivers in New Zealand. In 2008, Shijiazhuang Sanlu Group, the company's business partner in China, had to recall over 10,000 tons of infant milk formula that were found to have been contaminated with melamine, part of a broader industry-wide issue estimated to have affected over 300,000 babies and caused six deaths. So when the Kiwi firm recalled 38 tons of protein whey concentrate in China, Malaysia, Thailand, and other markets in August 2013 after tests had suggested (inaccurately, it later transpired) that they had become contaminated by bacteria that could cause botulism, Fonterra might have been expected to have been properly prepared to handle the fall-out. This proved not to be the case. An independent report later commissioned by Fonterra's directors into the incident described a "litany of failures at almost every stage," from inadequate product testing and tracking, slow escalation procedures and decision-making, a culture of "self-centeredness," and poor crisis management planning and communications.[1] The report also castigated Fonterra's use of social media as "immature" and singled out the firm's failure to communicate effectively online in China, where the issue had escalated at tremendous speed and where questions and comments went unanswered and rumors unchallenged.

The report also noted that Fonterra had outsourced its HQ's social media activities (as well as its broader social media activities in China) and found itself restricted to monitoring the reaction to the recall on social media manually. It had no crisis plan for the social web, had not trained its people, and its global corporate presence consisted of little more than a single Twitter profile and a LinkedIn page, both hardly used and neither showing any meaningful dialogue.

Developing a crisis plan for social media

Before we get into the nuts and bolts of how you should prepare for a crisis in social media it is worth considering what a "social media crisis" is. But first it is helpful to define "crisis". The Institute of

Public Relations defines a crisis as "A significant threat to operations that can have negative consequences if not handled properly" and which results in threats to public safety, financial loss, and reputation loss.[2] Crisis communications expert Steven Fink suggests a bone fide crisis only exists if each of the following questions are answered positively:[3]

1. Is the situation a precursor that risks escalating in intensity?
2. Does it risk coming under close scrutiny?
3. Will it interfere with normal business operations?
4. Will it jeopardize our public image or bottom line?

As we have seen, the great majority of negative situations in social media are not crises but relatively minor problems, slow-burning issues, or short, sharp incidents. A "social media crisis" exists no more than a radio crisis, a newspaper crisis, or a magazine crisis. A crisis is a crisis and, given its nature, plays out across any and all media.

Given that people at the social media coal face are often not crisis communications experts (or even communications professionals) but marketers, customer service representatives, online community managers, and agency juniors, it makes sense for companies to develop a plan that covers the broad range of negative situations they face online (which, in effect, includes all "offline" situations) and that can be used daily by the many different types of people involved one way or the other in developing, managing, and evaluating its online presence. This plan – let's call it a Social Media Crisis Plan – should include:

- Crisis and issues definitions
- Goals and measurement
- Online stakeholder and influencer lists
- Policies and protocols
- Content, channels, and tools

- Team, partners, and suppliers
- An appendix of examples.

We'll explore each of these below.

Crisis and issues definitions

As we saw in earlier chapters, the variety of negative situations facing organizations today is immense. Yet some of these threats are more likely to occur and, when they hit, are more dangerous than others. Like a traditional Crisis Plan, a Social Media Crisis Plan should set out three to five different categories of threats based on the likelihood of their happening and their impact (Table 14.1).

TABLE 14.1   Severity classification of reputation threats

LEVEL 5 - CRITICAL
- Extensive breach of customer or employee data
- Kidnapping of an employee
- Major damage to a firm's physical assets during an earthquake or terrorist operation.

LEVEL 4 - SEVERE
- Allegations of corruption amongst a firm's senior leadership
- External leak about serious and unexplained injuries to employees at work
- Threat of legal action by a major investor over the accuracy of a firm's financial statements.

LEVEL 3 - SIGNIFICANT
- Escalating allegations of use of child labor amongst a company's suppliers
- Community protests about local environmental damage
- Campaign by a global NGO to boycott a company's products.

LEVEL 2 - MODERATE
- An escalating online rumor about a controversial product ingredient
- A public complaint about a faulty product by a celebrity customer
- A backlash to an unexpected price increase or brand marketing campaign.

LEVEL 1 - LOW
- Known though uncontroversial concerns about a product circulating online
- Negative online feedback to a media article concerning employee compensation
- A one-off complaint on Facebook by a customer about poor quality product packaging.

Many crises start as lower level issues but go unnoticed, are ignored, or are allowed to escalate until they become high level crises. This has always been the case. But the internet and social media pose additional risks and can ignite even the most innocuous threats in quite unexpected ways. Much also depends on how an organization is seen to respond. Handled well, a Level 1 or 2 threat will remain as such; handled poorly it can quickly become a more daunting challenge.

Goals and measurement

It is important to be well prepared and to have a clear idea – or as clear as an idea as possible – of what you are likely to be trying to achieve when a crisis hits. Your business objectives may range from ending the situation as soon as possible, limiting financial loss, restricting potential lawsuits and regulatory penalties, protecting lives and minimizing the impact of the incident on the environment, or protecting the interests of your customers. At some point, you will also want to regain confidence and restore trust.

The standard mantra of crisis communications is to tell everything you know as soon as you know it. Social media can play a valuable role in communicating the latest updates and explaining complex issues without their being watered down or misinterpreted by the media. But there are also other ways social media can be used in a crisis, for which the objectives can be quite different. For example, social media can help governments and local authorities improve the *quality* of information available to the public in the aftermath of natural disasters, acts of terrorism, and other incidents through the bottom-up sharing of tweets, photographs, and location data. The Boston Police Department found that the outpouring of tweets, photographs, and video produced by the public during and after the Boston Marathon bombings helped it co-ordinate its response and track down the bombers. However, the deluge of information also complicated matters, especially as much of it was based on rumor and misinformation. Notoriously, members of Reddit were encouraged to come forward with "any and all theories" as to who did the bombings on the "findbostonbombers" discussion thread only to wrongly identify several people. Analyzing a rumor that an eight-year-old girl had died in the attack, University of Washington researchers identified 92,700 tweets mentioning her, of which 90,700 were classified as misinformation. The rumor was untrue, and only 2,000 tweets were ever corrected by those that had sent them.[4]

Once you have decided your overall goals, your Crisis Plan should set out specific objectives for each threat you have identified, from awareness of key company messages and the sentiment of online discussions to overall trust in the company and the strength of your relationships with important online influencers.

Online stakeholder and influencer lists

Online journalists, bloggers, highly networked online customers, activists, and others shape perceptions of organizations to a greater or lesser extent. Some may love your company and what it stands for and will support you through thick and thin, others are more cautious and withhold their opinions until they are confident they know the facts. A few will take any opportunity to drive a knife deep into your back. Whatever their perspective, it pays to know these stakeholders well in advance of a crisis, so you don't have to spend precious time identifying people and hoping they will say nice things about you. If you haven't already done so, you need to identify who these people are, where they spend their time online, and who they talk to, have professional relationships with, and are themselves influenced by. You should also understand their interests, track record in supporting or attacking you, and find out how credible and influential they are about the threats you have identified. Better still, you will already have built relationships with them.

Policies and protocols

With people going online the moment they hear of a crisis, you have to move like lightening to make sure your perspective is heard and work hard to make sure that what you say is consistent, sufficiently flexible to cope with frequently fast-changing situations, and appropriate to your various audiences' needs and expectations. To do this effectively you should develop policies and processes governing what you say and when and how you say it during a crisis.

Messaging

Social media enables you to talk with your audiences in a much more direct and human manner than through traditional media. It also enables you to talk about things you might not normally refer to in more formal statements – say, minor updates about meetings you are having with local authorities or for your CEO to express his personal feelings about the situation. But you must also ensure that whatever you say online is consistent with everything else you say and do. Responsibility for crisis messaging generally lies with your main Crisis Team; you will need to decide what degree of flexibility the Social Media Crisis Team can have.

First response

The first thing you say in a crisis sets the tone for everything you say afterwards, so it is essential you get it right. In traditional crises it is recommended that your first statement is issued within an hour of you hearing about the incident and should take the form of a short proclamation acknowledging the problem, stating you are actively looking into it, and expressing concern for whoever has been impacted. Approved by your Legal team, it effectively allows you to say something quickly while actually saying very little and not exposing you unduly to legal risks. With the social web now the first place people will start talking about an incident and the media increasingly taking their cue in a crisis as much from what's going on online as through their offline contacts, you are under pressure to say something within minutes on Twitter or Facebook before issuing a fuller, more formal statement to the media. And if you do go first in social media you'll be under real pressure to be honest and communicate in a normal human voice devoid of bland phraseology and legal fence-sitting. On the downside, as there is often no supporting information available very early in a crisis, taking to social media first can lead to unwanted speculation. Whichever way you jump, your Crisis Plan should include guidelines on whether and under what circumstances the social web is to be used to make your initial response and how quickly it should be made.

Ongoing external communications

Crisis communications is all about rebuilding trust as quickly and broadly as you possibly can. To do this effectively you'll need to be keeping your customers, the general public, local communities, and other audiences regularly in the loop on the latest developments and what you're doing to minimize the chances of something like it happening again. This requires thinking about which audiences the Social Media Crisis Team will be responsible for communicating with throughout the crisis (generally it will focus on customers but you will also need to consider whether it is appropriate for it to interact with more sensitive audiences such as activists and journalists) and who will approve what is said online.

Employee communications

As an outsider, it is easy to get the impression that organizations are largely preoccupied with protecting their external image in crises. In some instances this is a fair observation, which must be pretty galling when you are a long-standing employee and feel left out of the picture. Your people will be one of the most important audiences you deal with in a crisis, if not the most important (especially when they have been impacted directly) as they are – or should be – the best ambassadors for your firm. But with employees now easily able to question your integrity, deviate from, question, or, worse, contradict your official statements on Facebook or elsewhere, it is vital that your Social Media Crisis Plan provides guidance on whether your people are able to communicate externally on social media during a high profile negative situation.

Online influencers

Online journalists, bloggers, and heavy Tweeters may be very positive about your products and play an increasingly important role in how you market your firm. But they can also be totally unforgiving when things go wrong and it is important that interactions with these individuals are handled sensitively and in a manner that is consistent with your overall response. You will need to think about which online influencers should be prioritized, who is permitted to engage with them, and how they should be approached. Some organizations control access to their most important online influencers on an ongoing basis, for instance by insisting that marketing and product groups go through corporate communications. This is a sensible approach in a crisis when emotions run high and everyone has a point of view and when a normally objective and credible commentator can easily transform into a powerful adversary.

Online dialogue

I have worked with organizations that shudder at the thought of having to interact publicly with people on Facebook or elsewhere in the best of times and for which the idea of having to answer questions openly on the web during a crisis does not even bear thinking about. But listening to and participating in discussions on Facebook, Twitter, Weibo, and other platforms in times of trouble is not just expected of you but provides you with a great opportunity to explain your position, set the record straight, and build trust with individual users and with the community as a whole.

In Chapter 7 we explored using visibility, virality, sentiment, and influence to assess online discussions during negative incidents; these metrics also apply well in a crisis, though the thresholds will be set higher. You'll also need to think about who responds to questions online, how this is done, and how you are going to manage your official social media profiles at a time when things are particularly volatile.

- *Response approvals*. To whom should an online conversation be reported during a crisis? How should it be reported (email, word form, etc), and what information should be given to make the approval process quick and effective? And who should approve the response: the Crisis Team Leader or the Social Media Team Leader? Or will it require sign-off by the relevant topic experts in Public Affairs or in the business unit most directly impacted?
- *Who responds*. Who should respond to online conversations in a crisis? Should it be your core Social Media Team or the people managing your social media profiles and other online communities? Or should the core Crisis Team, Public Affairs, or a topic expert respond direct?
- *Response format*. What kind of response is appropriate? Should it be custom or pre-approved from a database? Should it link to further information and, if so, has your organization developed its own link shortener or does it use an off the shelf service such as bit.ly? In addition, should the responders identify themselves, on which channels, and using which convention (full name or initials)? Consider also how you might respond on different social media platforms. A response on Facebook may be different to one given on Twitter due to space restrictions on the micro-blog, whereas a response in a blog post can be much more detailed.
- *Conversation monitoring*. Online discussions do not necessarily stop when an intervention has been made or upon the apparent resolution of an issue, even less so in a crisis, so you should

consider for how long negative discussions are monitored after they been responded to. Often this is between 36 and 72 hours, though you may want to track a discussion with a top tier influencer over a longer period.

- *Deletions.* Should online conversations be archived during a crisis? In some circumstances, such as reported adverse effects to commercial drugs or in the event of criminal proceedings, you are legally obliged to archive all relevant communications, especially when they are made by aggrieved customers or other third parties. In other situations, it may simply be good practice to record online conversations so they can be accessed and referenced in the future.

- *Violations.* Online communities can become volatile, hostile, and unforgiving places in the midst of a serious incident. Tempers can easily get frayed, people may say offensive things to you or to others in the community, willfully misrepresent what you have done or said, or threaten your employees. If you haven't done so already, you need to consider what constitutes acceptable use of your official social media profiles and make sure they are monitored and policed carefully during a crisis. You should also be aware that deleting comments in the face of a hostile crowd is acceptable as long as the comments in question are clear violations of your own house rules or the platform's terms and conditions. But you should also note that the deletion of even a clear violation of your terms can backfire if the community has become overtly hostile. In these instances, you might consider privately warning the individual, followed by a public warning. If he continues to ignore you, you are then in a strong position to block him.

Local autonomy

In an ideal world your company will be able to respond to a crisis at a local level without having to rely on HQ to provide advice and support. Yet operations in smaller markets may not have the people and the skills necessary to take on the same responsibilities or to adopt identical policies and procedures. Your Social Media Crisis Plan should set out the degree of flexibility given to local markets to determine their own variations, clearly stating which policies and procedures are mandatory (such as the notification of Level 1–3 threats) and which can be localized.

Content, channels, and tools

Beyond defining what a crisis is and setting out the approval processes, your company's overall Crisis Plan will also set out how each threat is to be responded to from the outset in terms of the core messaging and overall communications approach. For the purposes of producing a practical and usable Social Media Crisis Plan it should be sufficient to set out the general guidelines and principles for preparing, distributing, and evaluating social media crisis communications without getting into the detail of how to respond to specific threats.

- *Content*. Your Social Media Crisis Plan should set out the kinds of content to be used online in a crisis and spell out how it will be used. For instance, a crisis holding statement is usually posted to a firm's social media profiles but ideally should not just be a simple copy and paste of the statement headline but a user-friendly summary. Your corporate blog and YouTube page are excellent channels for explaining context and spelling out your solution to the problem. Your plan should also set out how video and FAQs are to be used, and provide guidance on the use of keywords and hashtags to maximize online visibility.
- *Channels*. Many organizations use a wide spectrum of social media channels for corporate communications, brand marketing, and other purposes. Your Social Media Crisis Plan should set out which of these channels are to be used in a crisis and what they are to be used for. Twitter, for instance, due to its

character limitation, is useful for highlighting latest updates and addressing user concerns. Where these concerns are easily addressed, the user should be addressed publicly directly using their handle (@name) or directed to information already online using a corporate or third-party shortlink; where the question is less easily answered, the plan should spell out the appropriate response conventions for users that follow you and for those that do not follow you. You may also want to provide specific guidance for Facebook, YouTube, and Instagram, as well as for third-party channels such as message boards, customer review sites like TripAdvisor, consumer complaint sites such as Ripoff Report, and *Wikipedia*.

• *Tools*. There are any number of tools that can help you manage, monitor, and analyze your performance in social media during a crisis, from social media management services such as Salesforce. com's Buddy Media, Hootsuite, or Buffer, link shortening software such as Bit.ly or Ow.ly, and social media monitoring software such as Brandwatch, Percolate or Meltwater. Some of these tools contain workflow modules that enable you to define roles for team members, route draft posts to relevant team members or experts for approval, and pre-set priority keywords. Tools such as Lithium's Social Web also enable you to develop and store response templates that can be fine-tuned and used at a moment's notice. If your Social Media Team is already using these kinds of tools you will need to establish who will have access to them during a crisis and in what context they should be used.

Team, partners, and suppliers

Your plan should spell out who will handle a crisis in social media. Generally, this comes down to a question of resources and skills. Larger organizations have the luxury of dedicated teams and fatter budgets and can draw on additional specialized resources internally or externally. At small companies it may end up being the managing director or marketing director that leads from the front online.

The ideal Social Media Crisis Team will comprise people who know how to:

- Listen to and analyze online discussions
- Evaluate and develop social media campaigns and programs
- Manage online discussions, both on official social media profiles and third-party platforms
- Develop and distribute online content, including video
- Create and manage online advertising campaigns.

This mix of skills should be sufficient when a crisis hits. In addition, you may also want to involve people from your communications and perhaps also your marketing teams, some of whom may have strong social media skills. Make your call based on your crisis threat assessment and on the skills available. You'll also want to assign clear roles and responsibilities to each team member and figure out who the Social Media Crisis Team is going to report to. Given that social media is not usually represented formally on a firm's overarching Crisis Team or Committee, it is likely that the Social Media Team Lead will report direct to Communications or, in some organizations, to Marketing. You should also consider support – who will step into the social media listening role in a crisis if the relevant team member is on leave?

Your plan should also list important partners and suppliers involved in social media monitoring, online community management and moderation, and online media planning and buying, all of which may be required to support a crisis. Like your employees, these entities may need to be called in at a moment's notice in the middle of the night or over the weekend, so ensure that personal and work contact details are listed.

Appendix of examples

A Social Media Crisis Plan is both a reference document and an educational tool, so it is useful to add some examples of potential threats to your organization and how they should be handled. Each example might usefully describe the threat, note the Threat Level, set out the appropriate team members to be involved, the steps and protocols to be used, and illustrate the response, including the recommended holding statement, keywords, and hashtags.

Preparing your crisis team

Dwight D. Eisenhower reputedly said that "Plans are useless, but planning is useful." By which he meant that even the best laid plans will come unstuck in the fog of war and that the smartest shifts in approach are planned well in advance. While there's no substitute for experience, the best way of getting your team prepared for a crisis online is to simulate one.

A social media crisis simulation typically lasts half or a full day, with participants experiencing multiple phases of a crisis in a high-pressure environment. These sessions often focus on testing a team's ability to respond in a timely, consistent manner under duress and can be a useful way to assess the effectiveness of existing social media crisis guidelines and protocols. They are also helpful for gauging how well different teams work together under pressure.

* * *

As Eisenhower noted, all the preparation in the world counts for little against real experience. Something happens out of the blue or takes a dramatic turn and suddenly you are confronted with a slew of confused, frightened, and angry people desperate to understand what's happening. How you are seen to respond can make the difference between weathering the storm or going all hands down. In the next chapter we will look at how social media can be used to respond to a crisis, drawing on a number of recent examples from different industries and sectors.

chapter 15

Responding to a Crisis

On March 8, 2014, Malaysia Airlines (MAS) flight MH370 vanished into thin air. As I write this book, the plane is still missing and there is no convincing explanation as to what happened. Like many others, I found out about the tragedy on Twitter. The newswires and Malaysian media were running the plane's disappearance, people were talking about it online, and #PrayforMH370 was starting to trend. The internet was awash with nervousness and speculation, morphing over the hours and days and weeks into a cacophony of bewilderment and despair as the flight's trajectory was plotted and re-plotted and theories and counter-theories ran wild.

Of course, the circumstances of the MH370 disaster were exceptional. Commercial airplanes do not simply disappear. It was, and remains, to quote Winston Churchill, a riddle wrapped in a mystery inside an enigma. But the riddle was not helped by slow, confusing, sometimes contradictory, and frequently defensive communications by the airline and its government masters. Najib Razak, Prime Minister of Malaysia, later confessed in an article for the *Wall Street Journal* that "In the first few days after the plane disappeared, we were so focused on trying to find the aircraft that we did not prioritize our communications."[1]

To its credit, however, MAS did not run away from the internet hordes. Instead, it took to Twitter, Facebook, and Google+ to provide updates from day one. The airline swiftly launched an emergency "dark" website containing news releases, the passenger register, and emergency contact details. Digital marketing activities and promotions were suspended and the mastheads of its online properties blanked out. Yet there were also ways the airline's online response could have been improved.

With each situation different, it is difficult to make sweeping statements about how a crisis should be handled. Responding to a plane that has vanished into thin air is necessarily unlike a product recall, data breach, or an illicit love affair. Nevertheless, by analyzing how MAS handled its online response to MH370 alongside examples of organizations using social media effectively to respond to crises, it is possible to draw out some general principles that are applicable in a good number of scenarios.

Be fast rather than perfect

Warren Buffett advises the best way to resolve a crisis is to "Get it right, get it quick, get it out, and get it over."[2] With silence implying guilt, the sooner you can get the facts out the better. But this well-established cornerstone of effective crisis communications is also one of the most difficult to apply in practice: you find yourself dealing with a situation you did not expect, things are developing extremely fast and the information at your disposal is at best partial. So you end up publishing something that is legally acceptable but feels inadequate because it's all you have. And with Twitter alight and customers, bloggers, and trolls sounding off on your Facebook page you are under huge pressure to respond instantly.

Malaysia Airlines first lost contact with flight MH370 at 2.40am, but it was not until 7.24am that it confirmed publicly that the plane was lost and almost an hour later, at 8.13am, that it updated its social media profiles with the news. As the airline had already issued an official statement to the media, which immediately started reporting the issue, speculation about what might have happened to the plane had gone berserk on Twitter and Weibo. But the airline's voice was absent. By contrast, when flight MH17 disappeared over eastern Ukraine in July 2014, just a few months later, the airline's communications team took to Twitter to confirm it had lost contact with the plane an hour before issuing an official media statement.

Leading the response to a crisis on social media is a risky strategy when little is known about the problem. Speculation will run rife online and calls will immediately start flooding into your media center and customer support operations. And there's little useful you can say. Your people will be alarmed and want hard facts as soon as possible. Different parts of your business are unlikely to be up to speed on the issue so there's a good chance you will be communicating different messages to different audiences, any and all of which, in a crisis situation, stand a decent chance of being used on the record. On the other hand, you know before anyone else that the crisis has occurred and while you don't yet have the facts you figure that putting something out quickly will show you as honest and open.

This is not to say that using social media should always be the first line of communication in a crisis. There will be times when the situation is complex and requires considerable explanation, in which case it might be wiser to brief known and trusted journalists before making a public statement. Or when it is clear that an immediate apology is necessary, something that is hard to communicate effectively in 140 characters. That said, in many crises rumors and information will already be circulating on the social web. Like nature, information abhors a vacuum, and the longer you take to respond the more likely it is that rumors and misinformation will take root.

Moving first on the social web may not be the perfect solution but it sends a strong message that you are aware of the problem and are actively trying to sort it out. It also buys you precious time to start establishing the facts and to prepare a fuller statement.

Establish the appropriate social tone

What you say is just as important as how fast you move, and never more so than in the first hour of a crisis. In instances where the facts are unclear, a good first response to a crisis will acknowledge the situation, express concern for those impacted, and state the problem is being investigated thoroughly. It should also be expressed in a manner appropriate to the channel. An inherently conversational medium, social media demands a light, human touch, devoid of corporate speak and jargon. By contrast, Malaysia Airlines' first statement on Twitter in reaction to the MH370 incident simply re-published the header of the media statement it had earlier issued.

> MEDIA STATEMENT released at 7.24am/8 Mar 2014 – MH370 Incident – bit.ly/1kDkjiS

MAS continued to publish in this vein across all its social media channels for days after the plane first went missing. To its credit, the airline updated its online channels quickly and its online communications were clearly consistent with its offline communications. But its approach to social media failed to make best use of the medium. Contrast the airline's first response to MH370 with its response to the gunning down of MH17 a few months later, bearing in mind that MAS did not know the reason for the loss of contact with the latter plane at the time.

> Malaysia Airlines has lost contact of MH17 from Amsterdam. The last known position was over Ukrainian airspace. More details to follow.

For MH17, MAS also shifted its approach from providing a basic information service in a dry, corporate fashion to one that demonstrates concern, expresses sympathy, and speaks in a human voice.

> Our heartfelt condolences to the loved ones of those on board #MH17 Instagram.com/p/qnSeWmTOMl/
>
> From all of us here at @MAS, we would like to thank everyone for your continuous support during this difficult time. We greatly appreciate it.
>
> In light of #MH17, we'll be waiving any change fees for passengers who wish to make changes to their travel plan – http://bit.ly/MH17updates

Keep information flowing

The first hour of a crisis is a tense and chaotic period. Your Crisis Team has to come together and your Crisis Plan, centralized information systems, and business continuity plans activated. An initial assessment will need to carried out on the severity of the issue and the extent to which it will impact the day-to-day running of your business and on your organization's reputation. Almost immediately you have to start thinking about which of your various stakeholder audiences will need to be informed, what's going to be said, and when and how it will be communicated.

Issuing your first response statement is the first of many you will need to publish between discovering the problem, conducting a thorough investigation into its root cause, and deciding upon and announcing a solution. Throughout this period, which may last hours, days, weeks, or even months, the people directly and indirectly impacted by the issue will need to be kept up to speed on latest developments, and questions from the government, media, and local communities answered.

This may sound relatively straightforward, but if the facts are unclear, if technical experts disagree on the cause and solution, senior leaders have denied the problem even exists or are at loggerheads over who should be seen to act as spokesman, and the social media mob is calling for heads to roll, the job of keeping your audiences reassured and up to speed will be extremely demanding.

Malaysia Prime Minister Najib Razak was correct about the official communications response to the disappearance of MH370. It was slow, confusing, and suffered from a phalanx of spokespeople (from the PM and Acting Transport Minister to the CEO and various directors of the stricken airline) sometimes acting at cross-purposes, some of whom appeared not to have been trained for the media scrum. Little of this made the work of MAS' social media team any easier.

A commitment to honest, regular, and, wherever possible, useful communication by senior leaders is essential in a crisis. In contrast to Malaysia Airlines' labored efforts, the manner in which Buffer, a social media management service, handled a hack of its platform in October 2013 is instructive, not least as it happened over a weekend. At around 12.30pm Pacific Time, Buffer's platform was hacked and just under two hours later, at 2.20pm, its users started receiving spam tweets and Facebook posts to their personal and business accounts, apparently sent by Buffer itself. The spam posts were in fact mostly harmless but, had immediate action not been taken, Buffer would have left themselves exposed to significant reputational damage and potential legal recourse. The Buffer team acted swiftly and decisively. Twenty minutes after its users started being spammed and with complaints already circulating online, the company sent a tweet acknowledging it had been attacked:

> Hi all. So sorry, it looks like we've been compromised. Temporarily pausing all posts as we investigate. We'll update ASAP.

Over the next few hours Buffer CEO Joel Gascoigne and his team got stuck into finding out what had happened and identifying how they could stop the spam, secure their platform, and contain the fall-out that was spreading online, tasks made all the harder when the team was out of the office and operating virtually from eight locations across the world. Connected by video using Google Hangouts continuously throughout the incident, the team used its blog, Twitter, and Facebook profiles to communicate a series of updates on the status of their investigation, how they were addressing the problem, and providing advice to customers about what they could do to protect their accounts.

Within an hour, the CEO had sent an email to the company's one million-plus customers acknowledging and apologizing for the problem and advising them (myself included) how they could protect themselves. That email was followed by another 10 updates over the following 48 hours, all of which were emailed to customers, posted to the company's blog, and published on Twitter and Facebook. Helpfully, all its updates were also published to a single page on its blog so people could see the exact run of events.[3]

Update 2: 3pm PST

We've increased security for how store Twitter tokens and deployed a fix.

You can login with Twitter again. You will have to recon-nect all your Twitter accounts in Buffer. Here is how to reconnect them.

You can now send Tweets via Buffer again.

Update 3: 5:30pm PST

We're currently working directly with Facebook and AWS to get this all sorted out. It looks like we are making our way closer to a full recovery. Twitter (see Update 2 above) should be working again 100%.

About your Facebook posts: Currently it's not possible to connect or post to FB with Buffer. We hope to have this working again real soon for you and I greatly apologize for the hassles this might have created.

Update 4: 8pm PST – All posting is working again!

We've greatly increased the security of how we handle all social messages being posted and everything is back to normal. Please try signing into your Buffer account from http://bufferapp.com instead of the mobile apps for now.

For your Facebook account:

If you had Facebook posts via Buffer scheduled during the outage, they will likely appear as 'failed' in your Buffer queue. You can just hit 'retry in Buffer' and they should then be scheduled normally and go out as expected again.

For your Twitter account: You will have to reconnect all your Twitter accounts in order to start posting again. Here is how you can reconnect your Twitter account.

We're also going to publish an in-depth post about what the spammers got access to and what we did to fix it. In short, we encrypted all access tokens for Twitter and Facebook and also added other security measurements to make everything much more bullet proof. More on this in a coming post!

Update 5: 9:00am PST Sunday, 27th of October
We have monitored all behaviour overnight and everything has remained normal. All posts to Facebook and Twitter via Buffer should be going out normally. For Twitter you will have to reconnect your accounts from the web dashboard.

We have greatly increased security of how we are posting to Twitter and Facebook and have confidence to cover the security holes the hackers have used to break into our system.

What's next: We're working with several security experts on tracking down exactly how it was possible for the spammers to get into our system. We're making good progress on this, this morning. What will follow is that we're going to publish an in-depth update on the impact of the hack and everything we know about how it happened.

Buffer had a torrid experience over a few days but its responsiveness and determination to communicate regularly and honestly pulled it through to the extent that online complaints quickly subsided and were replaced by congratulations on how the team handled the situation. Some people even pledged publicly to shift their business to Buffer from its competitors.

Tell your story convincingly and make sure it gets heard

Faced with a crisis it is tempting to focus on what you're going to say rather than how you're going to say it. And this makes perfect sense – the facts are unclear, the media is on your back, and you are under huge pressure to push out a media statement quickly. But *how* you are going to tell your story is just as important as what you say, perhaps even more so given the breadth and intensity of emotions that crises give rise to and the fact that journalists and bloggers are constantly on the lookout for sound bites, photographs, video, and other visual elements to tell their stories.

If an image is worth 1,000 words in normal circumstances, in a crisis it is worth 10,000. Rightly or wrongly, a single image can become irrevocably connected with a crisis. BP's spill in the Gulf of Mexico is forever associated with a pelican covered in oil, its wings outstretched but incapable of flight. Think of 9/11 and there's the shot of the second plane angling into the South Tower of the World Trade Center while smoke billows out of the North Tower. Or the photograph of Goldman Sachs CEO Lloyd Blankfein giving testimony to the Financial Crisis Inquiry Commission in Washington DC, an indelible reminder of the chaos of the 2007–8 global financial meltdown.

Just as real care should be taken in a crisis to ensure that your company leaders are pictured in the appropriate place, wearing the appropriate clothes, and conveying an appropriately empathetic or focused demeanor, you must think carefully about how your story is going to be told online and how it will be discovered and experienced. Most obviously, materials can be re-used from your "offline" response activities: photographs of the damage to your product, annotated maps of the local topography, or video footage of your CEO speaking at a press conference. Or you can develop a basic chronology of events so that customers, journalists, and others can see exactly what happened and when, something done simply and effectively by Buffer when it listed all the updates to its customers about its data breach on a single page of its blog. How-to graphics can also work well. In its second update, Buffer included a simple annotated screenshot of its product showing customers how to protect and re-connect their accounts.

Buffer had to deal with a screen-based technical issue, something difficult to explain in an engaging manner. Other types of crises – airplane crashes, earthquakes, terrorist attacks, and poisoned customers – are more visual and pose significant challenges and opportunities for organizations on the receiving end. On the one hand, graphic images of actual or alleged misdemeanors place the burden of proof much more firmly in the hands of the supposedly guilty party. On the other hand, grisly images of contaminated products or gushing oil can act as a spur to establish a more human face to your company and to persuade audiences of your own case using storytelling techniques. BP's response to the Gulf of Mexico oil spill is widely derided for attempting to shift the blame onto its partners and for the tone-deafness of its then CEO Tony Hayward. It took the company four weeks after the crisis erupted to get to grips with social media. But when it finally did so, online storytelling was at the heart of its efforts.

The focus of the team responsible for developing and implementing BP's social media crisis strategy was two-fold: first, to tell BP's side of the story and, second, to address concerns and answer questions about the spill from local communities and the wider general public as openly as possible. To do this, a team of four worked out of BP's Crisis Command Center in Houston, drawing on a team of 57 people working in shifts in nine locations on two continents to develop between 20 and 24 stories a day for the oil firm's Twitter, Facebook, YouTube, and Flickr accounts.

There was plenty of work to do. BP's social media accounts had not been updated after the spill started on April 20 and then were restricted to official press statements and a few collections of photographs of environmental defense work, local community outreach activities, and its Crisis Command Center in Houston. The team's first task was to start providing regular factual information as quickly as possible about the status of ongoing efforts to cap the wellhead and contain damage to the environment. Breaking news was posted immediately online, in addition to simple, bullet-point Daily Operations Updates and extensive photographs of the emergency and clean-up operations. An online dashboard with live footage of the wellhead was developed and made publicly available on BP.com, quickly becoming the most viewed page on the site.

Much effort was also put into developing video and multimedia content. A corporate "roving reporter" with a Flip cam was assigned to tell the stories of people working on the response in community outreach offices and clean-up staging centers across the breadth of the Gulf region. The reporter was also given unrestricted access and permission to film meetings and interview engineers and executives at the firm's Crisis Command Center and posted these to YouTube. Detailed technical briefings were also made publicly available, such as BP Senior Vice President Kent Wells explaining complex technical details of the underwater operations in everyday language.

In the early stages of the crisis there were virtually no comments from the public on its social media accounts, but as soon as CEO Tony Hayward apologized for his infamous "I want my life back" statement on June 3 on TV, in full-page ads in the *New York Times*, the *Wall Street Journal*, *USA Today,* and the *Washington Post* as well as on Facebook, BP's online community took off. This was hugely helped by the fact that Haywood's Facebook contribution was referenced by news publications around the world, establishing the page as a credible news source and leading to a surge of online comments and questions. Hardly surprisingly, many of these comments were critical of BP, but the company's social media team was careful to let users vent while actively responding to questions to which it had the answers. It also hosted regular Facebook Q&A sessions with senior BP executives such as Mike Utsler and Dave Rainey of BP's Gulf Coast Restoration Organization (the unit set up to manage the firm's long-term response to the spill) (Figure 15.1).

Social media enabled BP to establish relationships and talk with people it would not have had access to, from local residents and fishermen to dolphin experts. But even after the surge in online

Answers to Your Questions - Mike Utsler, Chief Operating Officer of BP's Gulf Coast Restoration Organization

November 19, 2010 at 8:46am

Our Q&A session with Mike Utsler will begin shortly at 11:00 a.m. CT. Mike is the Chief Operating Officer for BP's Gulf Coast Restoration Organization (GCRO) and will be addressing your questions regarding BP's commitment to cleanup and restoration activities in the region, including initiatives on beaches and marshes. To see what Mike has to say to in response to commonly asked questions and those from Facebook users, **read below and refresh your page regularly for the most recent answers**.

Mike Utsler, COO of BP's Gulf Coast Restoration Organization

Note: Mike will answer questions previously submitted from Facebook users during this session. In the interest of legibility during this Q&A session, **please direct new questions or side discussions here:** http://on.fb.me/AskMikeNov19. We'd like this area to be reserved for users' questions and Mike's answers.

Learn more about the ongoing beach cleanup operations that are critical to Gulf restoration on BP.com: Cleanup-Beaches.

Like · Comment · Share

FIGURE 15.1 BP Gulf of Mexico oil spill Facebook Q&A

Source: BP America Facebook page.

followers as a result of the huge media interest in Tony Hayward's apology on Facebook, BP felt that its commitment to the region was not getting through to enough people. So it bought keywords on Google and other search engines such as "oil spill" and "gulf spill," supported by taglines such as "Learn more about how BP is helping" to send users to BP.com where they could witness the full range of its efforts, learn about volunteer opportunities, and how to file for claims.

Listen actively and be seen to be listening

As we have seen, BP made a substantial effort to answer public questions and concerns about the Gulf of Mexico oil spill. But in truth its focus was more on pushing out its story than being seen to be listening and fully participating in online conversations. And any attempt to be seen as listening was seriously stunted by the widespread perception, ingrained from the moment news of the disaster became public, that it was skewing information for its own purposes and was more interested in itself than those impacted by the spill. BP had lost credibility from the outset and was always going to face an uphill battle convincing people it cared about them.

Had local communities and others been convinced BP was listening and acting in their best interests from the get-go, it is highly unlikely it would have got itself into the mess it did. By contrast, when General Motors was planning how to communicate its imminent Chapter 11 bankruptcy filing in June 2009, the biggest Chapter 11 filing in history and the darkest day in GM's history, its social media team focused on answering questions from worried car owners and others immediately and openly, rather than treating it as an embarrassing if necessary exercise in damage limitation. Fully expecting an avalanche of complaints about the firm and its management, unions, and the US government bail-out process in general, the team resolved to answer everything that was thrown its way in an as accurate, unfiltered, and "un-spun" manner as they possibly could.[4]

They later worked out that between 75 and 80% of the tweets and posts they published over the week of the bankruptcy were in response to people's statements or questions, and that they had participated in over 2,500 online discussions. Rather than being seen as defensive, GM's online approach won widespread plaudits and prompted an Associated Press reporter to take to Twitter to note that "in the old days, a company would be hiding in a cave on a day like today."[5]

There's another advantage to focusing on interacting with your audiences rather than pushing out information: you are making it clear that they are important and that you are listening to them. Like all communications, crisis communications should be approached as a two-way process in which the expectations, requirements, and perceptions of stakeholders are assessed and acted upon. You should also be listening regularly to get a clear handle on how much support you have, where your support is coming from, and to gauge the reaction to your actions to address the problem. Traditionally media audits and stakeholder surveys would help you get a fix on these kinds of questions during a crisis; nowadays social media is a massive focus group that can be tapped instantly for insights and feedback.

Proactively rebut rumors and misinformation

Another advantage of online listening during a crisis is that it enables you to identify and track rumors. False, partially true or entirely true, the result of malicious intent, wishful thinking or misunderstanding, rumors are a fact of life in crises and, thanks to the internet and social media have become much more numerous and, with their sources unknown and traveling at high speed, can cause significant damage. However dealing with a rumor going viral on Twitter is fraught with danger at the best of times and is trickier still in a crisis when the stakes are that much higher. Here are some simple rules of thumb for managing rumors, misinformation, and disinformation circulating online during a crisis:

- **Untrue**. Crises attract rumors like a rotten carcass attracts fleas, a stench made even more acute by the ease with which conspiracy theorists, bored bloggers, and opportunistic competitors can now say something misleading or entirely untrue about you online. We saw in the last chapter how over 90% of tweets during the Boston Marathon bombings were misleading (albeit the great majority accidentally so). How you respond to untrue rumors will depend on the motivation and influence of those people spreading the rumor, and the potential impact of it being taken seriously. As a general principle, it is important to shoot down manifestly untrue rumors quickly, clearly, and unambiguously, especially when they are peddled by top bloggers, journalists, your business partners, employees, and other credible sources. If you do respond, make sure you have the facts to support your case, ideally in the form of photos, videos, or documents, all of which can be stored on your crisis website or your corporate blog. One way Obama's 2012 Presidential campaign tried to dispel false rumors was through a section on its main campaign website aimed at empowering its grassroots supporters to fight back against attacks, together with a purpose-built "Attack Watch" website focused on rebutting misleading political advertising. Make sure you also use a hashtag to make your response as visible as possible in the online news stream.
- **Partially true**. Most rumors in a crisis are neither completely untrue, nor wholly true, but start based on some element of fact and, like Chinese whispers, mutate as they are passed from

person to person. Of course the internet and the social web have hugely increased the scope for distortion as more and more people comment on, retweet, and share the latest version, making it difficult to know if you should intervene and, if so, where and when. Generally I advise clients not to respond to partially true rumors during a crisis, as intervening often only gives more credence and visibility to the most harmful part of the rumor. That said, it can be worth responding when the statement is based on a clear misunderstanding, thereby giving you the opportunity to look responsible and responsive. If you go this route you'll need to be able to substantiate your position. It also pays that your tone is helpful rather than blunt or hostile, which can easily be seen as defensive.

- **True**. While the great majority of rumors circulating online during crises are partially or entirely untrue, "true rumors" also exist and can rapidly gain traction, especially if they unambiguously demonstrate the facts or reveal corporate wrongdoing. If a fast circulating rumor is quickly substantiated by a video or photograph, it is advisable to confirm the truth as quickly as possible – the faster you act the more honest you appear and the more likely you are to be forgiven, however awful the crime. On the other hand, a rumor can also work in your favor and if you think this will help clarify the situation for the broader community you can confirm its veracity and publicly thank the user. Whichever route you go, remember that it pays to be skeptical about what you are seeing online: MH370 and other crises were plagued by tall stories and doctored photographs purporting to show the real facts.

- **Speculation**. Just as the internet can be awash with rumors during a crisis, there is usually also a lot of speculation about what might happen, especially if the facts are still unclear. As Tony Hayward discovered when he told reporters "the environmental impact of [the Mexico Gulf] disaster is likely to be very, very modest," companies seen to be endorsing or engaging in any

kind of speculation themselves during a major incident risk looking overly defensive, manipulative, desperate, or out of touch,
especially in the early stages when the facts are not yet clear.
Just as you should not respond to journalists taunting you with
their hypotheses, don't be tempted to stimulate, condone, or
deconstruct speculation online, much of which will die a natural
death anyway or be deconstructed by the crowd.

In some instances a high-profile, creative approach is required to
fast-escalating rumors. In one of the worst disasters of recent history, an earthquake and 15 meter tsunami hit northeastern Japan
in March 2011, leading to the meltdown of the Fukushima 1
Nuclear Power Plant, resulting in the evacuation of 160,000 people, and causing massive environmental damage. But the disaster
was not limited to Japan; it also led to a crisis of confidence in the
nuclear power energy in other countries. Germany and Switzerland
announced they would close all nuclear plants, and China delayed
approvals for new reactors. In the US, Gallup's annual environmental survey on the eve of the disaster had found that 57% of
Americans were "strongly or somewhat in favor" of nuclear energy
as a way of providing electricity to the US. Two weeks later, after
the Fukushima disaster, seven in ten Americans said they were concerned about a nuclear meltdown occurring in the US.

The Nuclear Energy Institute (NEI), the lobbying group for the
nuclear industry in the US, had the biggest crisis on its hands since
the partial meltdown at Three Mile Island in 1979, only this time
the crisis was playing out online as well as in the mainstream media
and the corridors of power in Washington. The mood online was
especially volatile, characterized by widespread concerns and mis-
conceptions about the safety of America's nuclear reactors, in part
stoked by an active anti-nuclear lobby, and notable for a paucity of
high-quality information and objective analysis.

To address these concerns and fill the information void, the NEI
set out to become the most credible and authoritative source of

information online about the nuclear industry in the US. According to Scott Peterson, the NEI's senior vice-president for communications, "It quickly became apparent that social media was driving public opinion and we needed to respond. Much of the commentary was misinformed, which was understandable given the lack of available information about Fukushima in the US. So we set out to fill the information void by educating the public as factually and transparently as possible."[6] So the NEI, in conjunction with my former colleagues at Burson-Marsteller developed a series of short videos simplifying complex topics such as how nuclear plants are designed and operated, how nuclear fuel is disposed of, and on safety levels of nuclear radiation.[7] These themes were also addressed in over 100 posts on the *NEI Nuclear Notes* blog and promoted to online journalists and influential bloggers by email and using the NEI's presence on Twitter.

The NEI also realized that authoritative, independent voices were required if it was to be seen as credible. Videos were created featuring top nuclear experts such as Lake Barrett, who led the Nuclear Regulatory Commission's investigation of the Three Mile Island accident, and Jeff Merrifield, a former member of the Nuclear Regulatory Commission. And when online discussions on topics such as radiation jumped, respected experts were brought in to provide their perspectives.

The NEI also took care to correct factual errors on the internet and in the mainstream media, especially when they were being made by highly networked policy organizations, journalists, and analysts. A good proportion of these errors were attributable to confusion about nuclear terminology, which could be markedly different in Japan. But not everyone wanted to be educated, and anti-nuclear activists and others gleefully took the opportunity to stoke widespread fears about radiation crossing the Pacific and were happy to misrepresent the facts when it suited them. In these instances, the NEI immediately and publicly rebuffed the allegation by stating the facts on the offending blog or on its own official social media profiles.

Peterson estimates that 90% of the NEI's digital efforts were spent on developing and pushing out information to educate the general public, helping satisfy a hunger for factual information and alleviating concerns. Visits to the NEI website rocketed 1000% and its videos were viewed and shared over 50,000 times in the first month. Videos were quoted directly in articles by the *New York Times* and other media outlets. A month after Fukushima, a Gallup poll showed faith in the safety of the US nuclear industry had swung back to 58%.[8]

* * *

The social web, then, is the new crisis front-line and one which senior leadership must be committed to being at the heart of your response. But like traditional crisis management, a crisis does not stop once the initial chaos has subsided; you then have to reassure people it's not going to happen again and get your business back up and running as normal. The next chapter will look at how social media can be used to persuade people you have learnt the lessons and will emerge better, stronger and wiser.

16

Recovering from a Crisis

Several weeks after the disappearance of flight MH370 the plane was still missing, families of the passengers and crew remained camped out at Kuala Lumpur and Beijing airports, passenger numbers had collapsed, and the company's share price was badly holed. Desperate to get the story off the front pages, the airline and the Malaysian government could only sit and watch as the search operation dragged on and rumors circulated about what might have happened.

At some point Malaysia Airlines had to convince people that it was safe to fly with them again and that investors should keep their faith. Putting the airline back on an even keel was surely Malaysia Prime Minister Najib Razak's aim when he announced on March 24, 2014, three weeks after the plane had first vanished that, based on data from British satellite firm Inmarsat, flight MH370 had ended in the southern Indian Ocean. The statement was an unequivocal signal to the families of the victims, the airline's employees, and to its customers and investors that it was now time for the awful tragedy to be put to one side and life to get back to business as usual.

Appealing as this may sound, a crisis doesn't just stop once the initial frenetic bout of media coverage and online noise subsides. You have to get to the root of the problem, ensure it never happens again, and get your business back up and running as normal. You also have to spend time re-building fractured relationships with customers and other stakeholders, the ultimate aim being to restore the trust and loyalty that people had in you before your crisis struck.

The social web is well geared to supporting crisis recovery, enabling you to appeal directly to your audiences and apologize, tell your side of the story, and give the inside view of what you're doing to sort the mess out. It is also a powerful tool for showing you are listening and getting people closely involved in the process of rebuilding your business. But it has to be handled with kid gloves.

Making an apology online

If warranted, a good place to start the process of re-building bridges with those impacted is by apologizing. But apologies in crises are notoriously two-edged swords. A convincing apology will persuade people that you care for their interests and can dampen the worst of the noise. But apologies can also easily come across as insincere or slippery, thereby turning an already horrible situation into a truly terrible one. They can also increase your exposure to legal action.

Until recently, corporate apologies were few and far between and, if they were made at all, were made privately. But now everyone seems to groveling publicly, from politicians (Governor Chris Christie over Bridgegate, Toronto former Mayor Rob Ford for substance abuse) and sportsmen (LeBron James for describing a journalist as "retarded") to celebrities (Lance Armstrong, Paula Deen) and CEOs (Gregg W. Steinhafel for Target's security breach, AOL's Tim Armstrong for firing an employee in public). Indeed public mea culpas have become so numerous that the *New York Times'* Andrew Ross Sorkin has taken to running an "Apology Watch" column.

What's with the apology obsession? Partly it can be put down to the fact that bad news is now a whole lot harder to hide, forcing us to confront ugly truths more quickly, partly as the media has become more demanding. In addition, as Congressman Anthony Weiner will testify, it is remarkably easy to do something stupid or say something mildly offensive or downright controversial online without thinking twice about it, only to be hung, drawn, and quartered by the online lynch mob and for which an apology appears an easy solution.

None of this means you must necessarily apologize every time you do something wrong. But just as making an apology has been a way of getting the media off your back, the social web now means you can confess your sins and repent in a ritual act of public contrition in 140 characters, clearing the air online and offline simultaneously in the process.

If only it were so easy – apologizing on Twitter or YouTube is arguably an even more double-edged sword than apologizing through the press, on TV, or to your employees on the factory floor. On the internet you are likely to be talking to people who probably don't know you personally and may know little about your company or the nature or context of the crisis. So you can easily be misunderstood or be seen as insincere. And if you are unclear, appear evasive, or are seen as insincere, the feedback is instantaneous and wholly unforgiving.

What, then, makes for an effective apology online during a crisis?

On October 3, 2012, the date of the first Presidential debate between Barack Obama and Mitt Romney, an offensive tweet referencing Obama's recently deceased grandmother Madelyn

Dunham was posted from KitchenAid's official Twitter account in the US to its 24,000-plus followers.

> Obamas gma even knew it was going 2 b bad! 'She died 3 days b4 he became president'. ??? Wow! #nbcpolitics

The message was immediately re-tweeted into social media infamy. But KitchenAid brand manager Cynthia Soledad acted quickly to delete the post and issue an apology.

> Hello, everyone. My name is Cynthia Soledad, and I am the head of the KitchenAid brand.
>
> Deepest apologies for an irresponsible tweet that is in no way a representation of the brand's opinion. #nbcpolitics
>
> I would like to personally apologize to President @BarackObama, his family and everyone on Twitter for the offensive tweet sent earlier.
>
> It was carelessly sent in error by a member of our Twitter team who, needless to say, won't be tweeting for us anymore.
>
> That said, I take full responsibility for my team. Thank you for hearing me out.

Faced with an instant crisis, Soledad hit all the right notes.

- She acted quickly and focused on Twitter, the channel where the problem had ignited.
- She personally took control, in her own name.
- She apologized sincerely and directly to Barack Obama and his family using the appropriate @name discussion convention.

- She distanced her company from the problem credibly while taking full responsibility for her team's transgression.
- Appropriate corrective action was taken immediately.
- She used plain language unvarnished by evasiveness or jargon.
- She didn't try to compress the statement into 140 characters.

Video is also a popular channel for expressing remorse. However, the visual and viral nature of YouTube significantly raises the stakes. On the plus side, it enables you to speak directly to your audience in a controlled environment and is a powerful way to appeal to your customers' emotions. On the downside, the camera never lies: an insincere or unconvincing apology is easy to spot and lives forever. And a woeful video mea culpa is a whole lot more likely to go viral than one that hits all the right notes.

When customers started complaining about the sheerness of Lululemon's yoga pants in March 2013, the firm's then CEO Catherine Day moved fast to recall the product and fired the firm's chief product officer. While the recall cost the company an estimated USD 67 million and wobbled its share price, customers and investors stuck with the firm. But founder Chip Wilson reignited the issue in an interview with Bloomberg TV several months later by blaming the shape of women's bodies for the see-through nature of the product.

Facing an uproar, Wilson took to YouTube. In his words:[1]

Hello, I'm Chip Wilson. I'm founder of Lululemon Athletica.

I'd like to talk with you today about the last few days of media that's occurred around the Bloomberg interview.

I'm sad, I'm really sad, I'm sad for the repercussions of my actions. I'm sad for the people at Lululemon who I care so much about that have really had to face the brunt of my actions.

I take responsibility for all that has occurred and the impact it has had on you. I am sorry to have put you all through this.

For all of you that have made Lululemon what it is today, I ask you to stay in the conversation that is above the fray. I ask you to prove that the culture that you have built cannot be chipped away.

Thank you.

In principle, using YouTube to motivate staffers is a sound strategy. It reminds employees that you care and it sends a message to the outside world that you are focused on sorting out the problem internally and that you are being candid in your communications. Publishing internal statements externally also reduces the leaks that inevitably come with saying one thing internally and another externally. But Wilson's effort backfired viciously. While he acknowledged the problem and took personal responsibility, his apology came across as half-hearted. Perhaps worse, Wilson came across as emotional and confused and his words suggest he was not fully in control of himself. The video led to a frenzy of incredulous media coverage and has since been viewed over 200,000 times on YouTube. A month later he resigned his role as Lululemon chairman.

Contrast the way JetBlue founder and CEO David Neeleman used video to apologize for the grounding of his airline. On Valentine's Day, March 2007, a massive snowstorm hit the Midwest and Northeast coast of the US, causing widespread chaos and leading to airlines across the country cancelling flights. But the storm hit

JetBlue worse than its competitors, resulting in several of its planes being stranded and passengers on one plane left sitting on the tarmac at New York's JFK airport for over 11 hours. JetBlue executives, notably David Neeleman, immediately apologized, promising to reimburse passengers and develop a plan to improve the way it handled operational difficulties.

Within a week the airline had developed an official Customer Bill of Rights setting out a slew of commitments to its passengers and confirming that these applied retroactively to those impacted by the Valentine's Day storm. Alongside an advertising campaign and round of media interviews, a letter of apology was emailed in Neeleman's name to affected JetBlue customers together with a link to the Bill of Rights document published on the airline's website. The letter also linked to an video hosted on YouTube and embedded within its corporate website in which Neeleman sets out its commitments going forward. [2]

Neeleman is clearly exhausted after a week of hyperactivity and little sleep. Bags show under his eyes. He is informal, wearing an open-necked shirt. He has no script, does not refer to notes and is clearly speaking without an autocue for his eyes don't once stray for guidance (unlike Chip Wilson, who clearly glances at a text). In places Neeleman mumbles and throughout he uses his hands as if to clarify his thoughts rather than illustrate what he is saying. And in this instance he does not apologize; this has already been done and the focus of the video is on how the airline is going to improve.

In short, Neeleman appears natural and sincere. And if the thousands of online comments (now disabled) made directly in response to the video are any indication, Neeleman managed to connect with his audience. And while many people vented their dissatisfaction, many more appeared swayed by his apparent sincerity and prepared to give JetBlue the benefit of the doubt.

Neeleman's informality and authenticity are worlds away from the spit and polish associated with many CEOs in a crisis and worked well in the context of a mid-tier US airline long associated with excellent customer service. But this approach may not work as well for every brand and in every situation. A CEO banker might be expected to act formally. In line with its conservative culture, Matthew Thornton III, senior VP of FedEx's Express US operations chose to wear a tie when he apologized on YouTube when its delivery man was caught hurling the PC monitor over a fence. And informality can be taken too far. Eurostar Chief Executive Richard Brown appeared not so much informal as disheveled when providing an update on a snow storm that left passengers stranded on trains between London and Paris in a tunnel beneath the English Channel.[3] One viewer suggested he looked "like a kidnap victim."

It is also essential to consider the broader cultural context. I often ask participants at my crisis workshops for their views on David Neeleman's performance and the responses are uncannily consistent: people educated in the west or who have worked for long periods in western or westernized companies usually say they identify with the JetBlue CEO and find his video believable and compelling. Yet the great majority of locals in Asia and the Middle-East say they find him bumbling and weak. Why? Because he jars with their perception of leaders as needing to be strongmen. Nor does his approach fit into Asia's more ritualized and formal culture of apology.

Bear in mind the following if you are going to apologize on YouTube:

- Have something concrete to say. Waffle is easily seen through on video, so wait until you know the facts of the situation or, better still, until you have agreed a solution to the problem.
- Start by introducing yourself and make it clear to whom you are addressing your apology.

- Get quickly to the apology and when you make it, keep it short and to the point. Don't try to bury your apology in a lengthy statement or obfuscate it using weasel words.
- Keep your statement short, if necessary using your corporate blog or website to explain the issue in more detail.
- Make sure what you say, how you say it, and how you appear are consistent with the values and culture of your organization.
- Be consistent about what you say in a crisis to all your audiences and assume that everything you say internally, not least on a transferable file such as video, is going to be leaked.
- Finally, don't lock down on negative feedback. Let your customers vent if that is what they feel like doing, listen carefully to what they are saying and, ideally, respond personally.

Re-building relationships

A well-judged, heartfelt apology can buy you some short-term breathing space in a crisis, but you also have to get your business back up to speed and persuade people that the actions you are taking to address the root cause of the problem are the *right* actions. Ultimately you have to restore the trust and loyalty that people had in you before your crisis struck. But people are disappointed, angered and hurt by your actions and are unlikely to take readily to you anytime soon. Worse, some relationships may have been fractured terminally – it doesn't much matter what you say or do, they will not hear or believe you under any circumstances.

Just as it takes perseverance to heal a fractured marriage, considerable time and effort has to be put into reassuring your stakeholders that you understand their concerns, are intent on repairing the damage, and are serious about changing for the better. Social media can be a powerful tool to support this effort but it has to be used carefully and appropriately.

I have argued throughout this book that the social web is best approached as a long-term investment in your brand and reputation rather than as a short-term marketing and promotional tool, and this is particularly the case when the world seems to be lined up against you. We saw in the last chapter how General Motors focused the immediate online response to its Chapter 11 bankruptcy on answering questions from its customers and the general public. And how, in the immediate aftermath of the Fukushima disaster in Japan, the Nuclear Energy Institute concentrated on providing factual information about the relative safety of nuclear energy in the US. To be sure, both organizations used social media to push out the latest news and information. But their real focus was elsewhere: on listening and responding, and on adding value rather than overtly protecting their reputations. In so doing they sent a clear message: they cared about their audiences.

Once you have persuaded people that you are acting in their best interest you have a much stronger chance of convincing them that you are learning from your mistakes and changing for the better. In his book *The Social Media Strategist* Christopher Barger recounts how General Motors, once it had weathered the storm of its bankruptcy filing and formally emerged from Chapter 11 protection six weeks later was finally in a position to re-focus on its products. It did not do this through advertising or aggressively pushing its cars on Facebook, but by giving 100 journalists special access to its existing and pipeline products as well as to the (new) company leadership at a special event in Detroit. To make the point that change was real and that GM was becoming a fresh and more accessible firm it also invited 100 "regular" people with whom the company had a relationship online. These were not just networked advocates; rather, a cross-section of American society was identified: a mix of supporters, skeptics, and cynics ranging from well-connected to auto bloggers to local students and moms with little online following from all over the country. And they were given the same level of access to the firm's products and leadership as the journalists, winning the company significant online plaudits but, more important, kick-starting the long-term process of persuading customers and the general public of the merits of the slimmer but revitalized GM in a meaningful and inclusive way.

Harnessing the crowd

The early stages of recovery are about re-building credibility and trust with your customers and stakeholders; it is also necessary to find ways to build on the progress you have made so that your business can get back on a firm footing. This requires broad support and it is at this stage of a crisis that marketing and advertising campaigns are often run. But real support is best achieved when people feel they are involved and have a stake in your recovery.

As we saw with the Boston Marathon bombings, people are naturally inclined to share information when innocent people are harmed in a public disaster. But the Boston bombings also taught us that a good deal of this information will be inaccurate or misleading, greatly complicating the initial response. For some, the risks of encouraging people to share photographs or leads or to plot information on maps out-weigh the benefits, at least in the early stages of a crisis. But others are more cautious. When a major landslide engulfed a rural neighborhood outside Oso, Washington state in March 2014, attempts to crowdsource photos and videos by local authorities did not initially work well because, according to then Snohomish County Deputy Director of Communications Bronlea Mishler, people were too busy helping with the response. Furthermore, she added in an interview for this book, "There are more risks than benefits to crowdsourcing, certainly when a disaster first breaks. Public bodies have a duty to be the trusted purveyors of correct and relevant information, which can easily be jeopardized by crowdsourcing."[4] In fact crowdsourcing worked much better after the initial turmoil of the slide had dampened. Particularly useful in this regard, Mishler notes, was a Facebook page set up by the authorities to help co-ordinate relief efforts and raise funds for the families of the victims. Importantly, local people, community organizations, and businesses were actively encouraged to share their thoughts, experiences, and offers of help, thereby increasing awareness of the disaster well beyond the 4,000-plus people who joined the community.

While crowdsourcing may appear a natural fit for public disasters, it is more challenging to harness the wisdom of crowds in a commercial context. Why would anyone want to come to the help of a global goliath that seems to care only about itself? Yet there are commercial incidents when involving the crowd can work well. For example, thousands of people freely donated their time and expertise to help Malaysia Airlines collect, verify, and interpret data about the missing flight MH370.

Dell has also been a notable recipient of online goodwill once it had used its mauling by blogger and journalist Jeff Jarvis in June 2005 to fundamentally re-engineer its approach to digital and social media and place listening and customer service at the heart of its efforts. First out of the gates in July 2006 was *Direct2Dell*, a blog platform intended to make the company more open to external audiences, help tell its own story and to engage customers and others direct. And then in response to a request by founder Michael Dell for his employees to figure out a way for the company to become more innovative, in February 2007 the firm launched IdeaStorm, an online community for customers and others to suggest and vote on product and service ideas. IdeaStorm quickly pulled in thousands of suggestions, the most popular of which was the idea that Dell notebooks should include the free Linux-based operating system Ubuntu. This recommendation was potentially controversial as it could easily have jeopardized the firm's long-standing relationship with Microsoft but Dell decided to pre-install the software any-way, sending a strong message that it was changing direction and re-building itself around its customers and their requirements. It worked: customer complaints declined, many of its most vocal crit-ics, including Jeff Jarvis, piped down, and the proportion of nega-tive blog posts about the company as a whole dropped from 49% to 22% within six months.

Crowdsourcing off the back of a series of crises is not necessarily for everyone. For such a model to be taken seriously you have to be open to criticism, be seen to be listening and learning, and be confident that your customers and other stakeholders will par-ticipate constructively rather than jump at an open opportunity to humiliate you. And you need to be seen to be putting in as much as you are taking. While Dell clearly listened to IdeaStorm and used the best ideas, it was also accused of not actively participating in the community, prompting it sometime later to hire one of its most vocal community critics, Cy Jervis, to become IdeaStorm's commu-nity manager, a position he holds to this day. As I write this book, over 23,000 ideas have been submitted, nearly 750,000 votes cast, 101,000-plus comments, and almost 550 ideas adopted.[5]

Reinforcing your online gateways

Most of the focus of this book has been about social media, yet search engines also play an important role in a crisis. When a crisis first breaks, rumors, opinion, and facts travel fast and furiously into the nooks and crannies of the internet, reaching workers and commuters and students wherever they are at that moment through their PCs or mobile devices. The drama of a major crisis combined with the power of the social web ensures the news finds its customers. But as the initial drama dies down and the crisis evolves and matures, people shift from letting the news find them to getting their updates from their favorite sources, be it their newspaper, TV or radio station, from their friends on Whatsapp, or through Google. A major crisis means TV viewership soars, newspaper website traffic and social media mentions go through the roof. Internet searches also bounce, as we can see from the volume of searches on Google.com for the term "oil spill"' during BP's Gulf of Mexico disaster (Figure 16.1).

As we can see from the chart, searches for news and information about the spill rose dramatically the moment the crisis erupted and near doubled as more people become aware of the problem and sought to understand what was happening. When the crisis died down and the media in all its forms turned its attention elsewhere, the number of searches declined rapidly. But they won't die out altogether, and search engines will remain a popular way of accessing information about the problem. Thanks to Google, information about a crisis remains online forever.

With an estimated 90% of search engine users relying on the first page of results, you will want the first 10 results to be in your favor. But in a crisis the top page of results for a search on your company or brand name will be dominated by negative news articles, comments, photos, and videos. And this will be the case

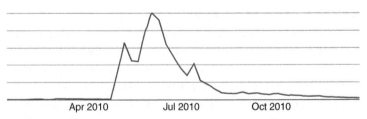

FIGURE 16.1 Searches for the term "oil spill" during BP's Deepwater Horizon crisis

Source: Google Trends.

during the crisis and for some time afterwards. Here are some tips for cleaning up your search reputation in the wake of a major meltdown.

- **Know your objectives**. Before getting your fingers dirty optimizing your online content for Google you need to understand what you are trying to do. This can be done by identifying the terms that people are using to find information related to your crisis and establishing which you need to minimize and strengthen.
- **Think laterally**. BP's crisis was about oil pollution. But it was also about local communities, fishing, beaches, conservation, and many other things. So don't think just about the terms directly related to your crisis but also about its broader impact. Also consider negative words and phrases directly associated with your crisis that may be being used to tarnish you online.
- **Think visually**. Google incorporates graphics, photos, and video in its default search results, and with visual content catching the eye quicker and able to tell a more instantly powerful story than text, special attention should be paid to considering how to push harmful imagery down the rankings and replace it with strong visual content that tells your story.
- **Focus on high-authority channels**. Whether you like it or not your online reputation is likely to be shaped by others, and due to the emphasis search engines now place on "authoritative" sources, the most visible voices about your crisis will be from the mainstream media and influential bloggers. But these are hard to displace; instead you should harness your energies on improving how they perceive and write about you.
- **Distribute content widely**. Understand which social media platforms Google ranks particularly highly and make sure your "owned" channels are constantly updated with the relevant messages and content, all of which is appropriately tagged and headlined. The more official online points of access you have, the

better the chance of improving your search engine reputation. And the longer you have had them in place, the more likely they are to have gained traction with search engines and audiences. As we saw in the last chapter with BP, buying keywords on search engines can help get the message out quickly and broadly.

- **Create a dedicated crisis hub**. One of the benefits of having an online hub housing news and information on your crisis is that search engines will find your information more easily and that means you stand to gain greater online share of voice. But you should also make sure that the site has its own URL and has been submitted for indexing to all the top search engines. Conduct a search connected with General Motors' recent ignition recall and you will more than likely be shown GMignitionupdate.com high in the top two or three results.
- **Maximize your recovery**. As we can see from Figure 16.1 search volumes do not spike immediately a crisis breaks but a little later as people return looking for context and meaning. So while coverage about your crisis in top newspapers will show up immediately in the search rankings, additions to your own website and other online channels may take days or weeks to show up. Rather than trying to nudge Google's results through your own channels early in a crisis, when coverage is likely to be negative, focus instead on ensuring the more positive nature of your recovery message is visible.
- **Know what not to optimize**. There may be some things that are said or done that you'd prefer the world not to know about, or for as few people as possible to know about. Optimizing is often thought of as being a must-have for all content, but it is just as important to know which messages and content you'd prefer search engines to find less easily.
- **Take the long view**. Just as a tarnished reputation cannot be restored in a day in the real-world, neither can it be re-built overnight on Google. Optimizing content for search engines is slow, laborious work and, with the top search engines regularly

updating their algorithms, you may find yourself having to start again more or less from scratch. Be patient!

* * *

The Chinese say that a crisis is both danger and opportunity. It can knock you for six but is also, like a snake shedding its skin, a chance to purify and renew oneself. As such, crises should be approached as opportunities to look both inwards and outwards and to reflect on where you've gone wrong and how you can improve. A crisis can also provide valuable insights into your enemy and the strength of your defense the battlefield. And with the social web now a fixed part of the terrain it is no accident that it often takes a serious incident for a CEO to wake up and smell the coffee. Of course, nobody likes being forced to change and it is your job to make sure this doesn't happen. But if it does, grab the bull by the horns and use social for what it is good at – providing rich insights into your customers and stakeholders and the opportunity to build truly strong, mutually beneficial relationships.

Epilogue

Remember the national tourism board that figured a good way of persuading tourists and businesspeople to visit its shores during a terrorist insurgency was to bury negative news on search engines and replace it with positive online views? The one that wanted to "create barriers to any future negativity relating to the security issues and any other crises," in short, to make it harder for negative opinion to be published and, if it did make it online, to limit its visibility and traction?

The country is Kenya and the event that forced itself into the global collective conscious was Al-Shabaab's siege of the Westgate shopping mall in September 2013 in which 67 people died.

Westgate was only the latest of a series of incidents since the US embassy bombings five years earlier, but rather than learning the lessons and preparing properly the authorities were again caught napping, awoke to a nasty jolt, and then tried desperately to close the digital barn door after the horse had bolted. Unsurprisingly their efforts to game Google and the social web were in vain – having fallen by a single digit percentage in 2013, the number of tourists visiting the country fell 40% during 2014.

* * *

Hopefully by now you have been persuaded that it is both necessary and possible to manage and defend your reputation online. Necessary as everything you say or do, whether it is in the real world or triggered by something you do online shapes how people see you and can shift and escalate at the blink of an eye. Little was ever gained by sticking one's head in the sand when something goes astray but now it is absolutely critical that you acknowledge and tackle the problem quickly and openly or it will be half-way round the world in a nanosecond.

That's not to say formulating the right response is straightforward and, as we have seen, some scenarios demand an orchestrated, multi-disciplinary effort involving the latest tools, techniques, and intelligence. Yet more often than not, managing and defending your firm's online reputation requires little more than a dose of common sense combined with good judgment based on experience. To end with, here are seven tips I have learned along the way that should help you to handle the jabs and jolts of the social web.

1. Know where you're going

It sounds obvious that every organization should have a clear understanding of the risks of the social web. However far too frequently I meet firms yet to think through how they're going to manage these in any meaningful way. Having a Q&A for when your latest campaign backfires is just not sufficient. Going through a systematic process of identifying and evaluating the threats will give you a good idea of what's likely to go wrong and provide a basis for developing a clear, practical plan.

Given the wide range of threats online and their potentially deep impact, I recommend you conduct your assessment as part of a comprehensive annual or half-yearly business risk assessment, making sure to include internal audit, corporate affairs, IT, HR, marketing, communications, and other relevant functions. If you are starting out on the social web or thinking of reconfiguring your approach, you can also conduct a standalone social media risk assessment.

There are many tools and techniques that you can use to identify the threats and determine their likelihood and impact on your business and reputation. These include one-on-one interviews and surveys, open-source intelligence, social media listening and topic analysis, extending to pattern recognition and scenario planning for more complex, forward-looking tasks, such as assessing emerging trends. Which you use will vary according to the scope of the exercise, the nature of the threat, and whether it is, to use Donald Rumsfeld's terminology, a *known known* (for example, high carbon emissions or product quality or customer service issues), a *known unknown* (such as the propensity for environmental groups and stakeholder opinion-formers to attack you using the internet and the social web), or an *unknown unknown* (unexpected big picture societal and consumer trends or the potential for "black swan" events). Each threat should then be prioritized.

You will also need to set clear objectives and metrics. Above all, it is essential that your metrics are useful and actionable. For example, sentiment is only moderately useful as a gauge of how people see and talk about you online; advocacy is arguably more useful as it indicates actual behavior. Or you can find a half-way house. HSBC, for example, classifies online mentions about the firm and its activities as "active criticism," "passive criticism," "passive advocacy," and "active advocacy." While it is much more challenging and time-consuming to classify these kinds of criteria by different types of audiences, this kind of approach is useful from a reputation defense perspective as it helps show where the real problems are and gives a better impression of the range of emotions and behaviors than many other approaches.

You should also ensure your senior leaders are kept abreast of your performance in social media. Often reporting is monthly or quarterly. Another idea is to circulate a daily summary of online mentions of your firm or of top issues relating to your industry, along the lines of the daily summary of important mainstream media coverage than many senior leaders still receive. Ensuring senior leaders are right up to speed on what's going on online is important as they are ultimately responsible for your firm's reputation, and social media provides a rich and timely insight into what people think about you, as well as a heads-up on potential problems before they hit the mainstream media.

2. Prepare to move fast and with precision and finesse

As first expounded in the classic *Inner Classic Theory of the Yellow Emperor,* one of the basic tenets of Traditional Chinese medicine (or "TCM") is that a long and fruitful life depends largely on a rational diet, regular habits, exercise, and a positive mindset, as opposed to pills and surgery. Actually the effectiveness of TCM remains largely unproven. But the Chinese must be doing something right, for despite the pollution, widespread smoking and drinking, and the lack of a national healthcare system and insurance scheme, the country boasts the largest population in the world and life expectancy significantly above the global average.

Companies would do well to take a similarly preventive approach to immunizing themselves against online disease. There are a wide range of actions that can be taken, from strengthening IT systems and front-line social media and customer service teams, ensuring compliance with the latest national laws and industry codes governing social media, and developing protocols governing employee behavior in social media and making sure these are fully understood and lived day in, day out. The beating heart of every firm's defense should be a system that tracks known threats online, identifies emerging issues, and flags potential problems, based on the kinds of criteria outlined in Chapter 7, and ensures they are routed to the appropriate individual or team for immediate assessment.

Yet however comprehensive the safeguards you put in place, you will never be fully protected from things going wrong, and when everything is real-time and the news cycle more or less instantaneous, it is essential you are able to take decisions quickly, surgically, and appropriately. Fortunately the great majority of problems online can be handled by your social media, customer service, and other teams at the online coal-face. However, as we have seen, some issues are more complex and require more thought before anything substantial is said in public, while others such as negative reviews or accusations by top tier bloggers and journalists, or anonymous and pseudonymous attacks by competitors or aggrieved employees, require particularly deft handling.

In these instances, you might consider setting up a rapid rebuttal team trained to hit back immediately on identified topics and issues (something that an increasing number firms are adapting from the world of political campaigning) or creating a special team to handle ongoing questions about more complex or contentious topics, such as those relating to climate change or public policy. Typically such "special situation teams" comprise topic experts with representatives from corporate affairs and communications, and are often run in-house. Where serious allegations are being made anonymously or pseudonymously, you might also want to set up or hire a specialist digital incident response team comprising communications, legal, and investigative experts to work closely together, able to trace IP addresses and map out the appropriate legal and communications response.

3. Commit to transparency but understand your limits

Openness, it is often said, is the price of entry to the social web. There much in this: the culture of the social web demands you disclose your identity and affiliation, rewards openness, and routinely outs subterfuge and phoniness. But transparency is not absolute and depends on the user and the context. Expectations of how government and big institutions behave and communicate differ markedly across the world. Multinationals in China, for example, are generally more trusted than local firms but are also expected to have higher quality products, better customer service, and to be more responsive and open when things go wrong. I have advised Chinese firms that regard subterfuge on the web as a necessity and certainly no evil. Equally ethical gray areas on the web such as newsjacking, advertorials (aka "native advertising") or even ghostwriting can be one man's meat and another man's poison.

Each organization should develop its own approach to transparency. At the very least, you will want to develop a policy that identifies who is allowed to represent your firm publicly online and how they should identify themselves, and consider whether this should be extended to your franchisees, business partners, and suppliers. You should also think through what you are prepared to say publicly for each of the threats you have identified in your risk assessment. At a minimum, you should agree on a basic holding statement for each threat. But you might also want to think carefully about your bottom line, making sure you have enough wiggle-room for the inevitable questions that come with being online.

More broadly, you would do well to consider how you intend to reconcile the need for compliance and the ad hoc release of information as circumstances dictate with the kind of proactive, total openness that the web rewards. The latter could involve commenting more regularly on industry and economic trends, providing more of a "real," warts-and-all inside view of the company, having your CEO and other senior leaders not just posting on Twitter but also answering questions, or proactively asking people on the web and in your online communities to ask questions and contribute ideas.

However, transparency is more than about social media, even if the social web is playing a key role in making organizations more accountable. Ideally you should consider the social web as part of developing a broader transparency strategy that includes communications, reporting, information sharing, and IT security. For example, given the scope for leaks and the use of internal social tools like Yammer and Chatter, you should ask yourself to what extent should information be allowed to flow inside your organization and how you are defining and keeping truly confidential information from being accessed and shared by the wrong people. You'll also need to bear in mind that the internet is global, so whatever you do and whatever you say in Wuhan, China, can instantly impact how you are seen in London and vice-versa.

4. Walk the talk with confidence but not arrogance

Like transparency, authenticity is a much flaunted but ill-defined part of the social media canon. Often it is portrayed as concerning "tone" and directs that you should be optimistic, friendly, accessible, open, and sincere, as opposed to defensive, evasive, single-minded, and overly polished, and that by doing so you will "humanize" your firm and build trust, and people will be more likely to give you the benefit of the doubt in times of trouble.

More important, authenticity is about making sure that what you say about yourself fits with who you actually are, that rhetoric meets reality. This means having a clear vision, purpose, and set of values and ensuring that these are lived and breathed by your people at all times, including during their downtime. It is also about ensuring these are understood externally and are driven consistently though all your communications.

It is also about being aware that "authenticity" is not risk free, and preparing accordingly. At one level, this requires understanding your suitability for social media. It is well established that organizations that are flat, prepared to take risks, and value innovation are better suited to the vagaries of the social web and the need for real-time communication than those that are hierarchical, slow, and risk averse. If by nature you are reserved and rather reluctant to open up, then it is probably unwise to participate too deeply or get involved in open-ended discussions on Twitter. On the other hand, the more you open up, the more scrutiny you will invite, especially if you are a well-known firm. Equally if you are seen to stand for something controversial or are seen as dogmatic, insensitive to other's opinions, or arrogant there's always the danger that someone is going to disagree with you or take offence. Living and breathing authenticity can require a thick skin online.

5. Listen with your ears, eyes, and heart and not with your mouth

Just about any communications professional will tell you that social media starts and ends with listening. Listening should underpin everything you do online, informing your overall approach to the social web, the tone and timing of your contributions, and the way you go about conducting your relationships. And listening is critical for managing and protecting your reputation, enabling you to detect and track known and emerging problems. However, listening well is easier said than done. In real life, we are all too easily distracted by other apparently more interesting things or are more focused on thinking of the next smart thing we can say than paying attention to what's being said. Indeed listening is frequently cited as the number one problem in communication; Amazon.com lists a mind-boggling 35,916 books on "listening skills" under a raft a categories, from communications and interpersonal relationships to psychology, motivational management, and leadership.

The internet has only made a bad problem worse by further lowering our attention spans. But online discussions also present their own, specific challenges. The sheer volume of data makes it difficult to understand what's relevant and important, the algorithms used to interpret conversations are imperfect, we cannot study someone's eye movement and body language on Twitter. Nonetheless, the basic principles of listening remain much the same irrespective of the channel or form. Real or "active" listening is about using our ears, eyes, and heart and demands our undivided attention. And it is about not jumping to conclusions too quickly, demonstrating empathy, and not interrupting when the other person is speaking. Yes, it is important to act quickly online but, as we saw in Part II of this book, it is just as important that you have a good fix on the underlying feelings and motivations of the user and read between the lines for what may be left unsaid before rushing to make a response.

6. Be spontaneous, creative, and make mistakes

Throughout this book I have argued for a systematic approach to identifying, evaluating, and managing the risks of social media, using data wherever possible to harness insights and your Social Media Crisis Plan and other playbooks to underpin your response.

But social media is as much an art as a science and it is important in a space as fast moving and open ended as the social web not to get too bogged down by rules and bureaucracy. Nor is it appropriate to stay religiously on message in an environment that demands the human voice and an empathetic ear.

While the social web is still evolving and the defense playbook, while filling out, is certainly not yet complete – it if ever will be – over time you will discover that many online incidents can be resolved and contained simply by moving fast and being open. There's often not much else you need to do. That said, there will be times when a little spontaneity and creativity does wonders to alleviate a bad situation. Instead of responding to a complaint or criticism in words on Facebook, why not do the unexpected and surprise your audience by shooting a short video telling your side of the story or by illustrating your perspective graphically. And be prepared to make mistakes – a little vulnerability is, after all, a basic human condition that everyone can relate to and understand, provided you are seen to learn from it. As Mark Twain is alleged to have said, "Good judgement is the result of experience and experience the result of bad judgement."

7. Understand what online reputation isn't and can't fix

Amidst the hype about social media you could be forgiven for thinking Facebook and Twitter are the answer to the world's problems. Yes, the social web is changing marketplaces, having a profound impact on the way companies are seen, and is a great platform for reaching new people and driving deeper loyalty. But that doesn't make it the answer to everything, Douglas Adams' number 42 for the internet age. All the tricks under the sun will never transform a me-too product into a viral hit. And, by the same token, if you've got a problem – a flaw in your character or weakness in your defenses – there's not much Facebook and Twitter can do to help; in fact they are only likely to make matters worse as people are going to talk about it in public. Instead you've got to focus on fixing the problem itself, while also ensuring that your business is run competently and ethically and that you have built strong, mutually beneficial relationships with your customers and stakeholders.

It is also tempting to consider your online reputation *as* your reputation, a kind of mirror image of what people think about you in the real world. Tempting, but mistaken. An organization's reputation is the sum of how many different stakeholders view it, from customers, employees, and investors to government, investors, and suppliers, each of which can have very different expectations. But online conversations are usually dominated by discussions about products and services by customers and prospective customers, while other stakeholder opinions are voiced less frequently. When was the last time you heard a high-level regulator, pension fund manager, or buy-side analyst actively discussing a company on Facebook? Social media is certainly a reasonable and timely indicator of your broader reputation *from a customer or general public perspective* but that doesn't mean it should be treated as an accurate or comprehensive reflection of the full range of views about you. The best way to get to know someone, understand their interests and expectations, observe how they live their lives, and to resolve problems remains face-to-face, in the flesh. The more clearly we understand the strengths and weaknesses of the social web and its relationship with other mediums, the more likely we are to use it effectively, reducing the chance we'll expose ourselves unnecessarily or make a hash of our response.

* * *

Now it's over to you. Good luck!

I'd love to hear how you get on. Please do connect with me online to share your experiences. You can also register to receive regular updates on online reputation trends and techniques at http:// charliepownall.com. By registering you'll also get free access to regular observations and tips as well as a raft of proprietary resources.

Notes

Prologue

1 Jeff Jarvis, *My Dell Hell* – August 29, 2005 http://www.theguardian.com/technology/2005/aug/29/mondaymediasection.blogging

1. The New Abnormal

1. Comcast subreddit - http://www.reddit.com/r/comcast
2. Pew Research Center, *Public Trust in Government 1958–2014* – November 13, 2014 http://www.people-press.org/2014/11/13/public-trust-in-government/
3. Edelman, *2014 Trust Barometer* – January 2014 http://www.edelman.com/insights/intellectual-property/2014-edelman-trust-barometer/
4. General Mills, *We've Listened – And We're Changing Our Legal Terms Back* – April 19, 2014 http://www.blog.generalmills.com/2014/04/weve-listened-and-were-changing-our-legal-terms-back-to-what-they-were/
5. Business Insider, *Business Insider Is Now Bigger Than The Wall Street Journal* – January 31, 2014 http://www.businessinsider.com/business-insider-2014-1

2. Defining Online Reputation Threats

1. AMR/Reputation Institute, *2012 Corporate Reputation Index* – May 2012 http://www.marketingmag.com.au/news/reputation-index-apple-rules-qantas-slides-telstra-jumps-13327

2. Australian Business Traveller, *Virgin Australia Leads Qantas in Traveller Satisfaction Survey* – October 2012 http://www.ausbt.com.au/virgin-australia-leads-qantas-in-traveller-satisfaction-survey

3. Ryan Holiday, *Trust Me, I'm Lying* (Portfolio/Penguin, 2012).

4. Altimeter Group, *Guarding the Social Gates* – August 2012 http://www.altimetergroup.com/research/reports/social-media-risk-management

3.   Strategic and Financial Threats

1. Brookings Institution, *The ISIS Twitter Census* – March 2015 http://www.brookings.edu/research/papers/2015/03/isis-twitter-census-berger-morgan

2. Deloitte/Forbes Insights, *Aftershock. Adjusting To The New World Of Risk Management* – June 2012 http://www.forbes.com/forbesinsights/risk_management_2012/

3. Charlene Li, Josh Benioff, *Marketing In The Groundswell* (Harvard Business Review Press, 2008)

4. McKinsey & Company, *Transforming The Business Through Social Tools* – January 2015 http://www.mckinsey.com/Insights/High_Tech_Telecoms_Internet/Transforming_the_business_through_social_tools

5. McKinsey Quarterly, *Capturing Business Value with Social Technologies* – November 2012 http://www.mckinsey.com/insights/high_tech_telecoms_internet/capturing_business_value_with_social_technologies

6. Clifford Chance, *View From The Top. A Board-Level Perspective On Current Business Risks* – 2014 http://www.cliffordchance.com/thought_leadership/global_risk_report.html

7. Deloitte, *Reputation@Risk. 2014 Global Survey On Reputation Risk* – October 2014 https://www.deloittereputationrisksurvey.com

8. U.S. Department of Defense, News Briefing – Secretary Rumsfeld & Gen Myers – February 12, 2002

9. Ximena Beltran, *Telephone interview with the author* – April 18, 2014

4.   Social and Environmental Threats

1. Reuters, *Bank Transfer Day Saw 600,000 People Switch* – January 27, 2012   http://www.reuters.com/article/2012/01/27/us-bank-transfer-idUSTRE80Q1TU20120127

2. Wikipedia, *Non-governmental Organization* – Retrieved on May 10, 2015
3. Sourav Roy, World Wildlife Fund, *In Person Interview With The Author* – April 2014
4. Jeff Sonderman, Poynter.org, *Journalists Beware: Shell Arctic Hoax Signals Move From Subtle Spin To Activist Deception* – July 19, 2012 http://www.poynter.org/latest-news/making-sense-of-news/181706/journalists-beware-shell-arctic-hoax-signals-move-from-subtle-spin-to-activist-deception/
5. South China Morning Post, *Shark Fin Trade From Hong Kong To China Drops Almost 90% In One Year* – April 8, 2014 http://www.scmp.com/news/hong-kong/article/1469412/hong-kong-shark-fin-imports-fall-35pc
6. Forbes, *#McDStories: When A Hashtag Becomes A Bashtag* – January 24, 2014 http://www.forbes.com/sites/kashmirhill/2012/01/24/mcdstories-when-a-hashtag-becomes-a-bashtag/
7. The New York Times, *Activists Try To Hijack Promotions By Sponsors of Sochi Olympics* – January 1, 2014 http://www.nytimes.com/2014/01/28/business/media/activists-try-to-hijack-promotions-by-sponsors-of-sochi-olympics.html
8. Tom Liacas, *Email Interview With The Author* – August 2013

5.   Behavioral and Legal Threats

1. Freshfields Bruckhaus Deringer, *Containing A Crisis* – November 2013
2. The Huffington Post, *Amy's Bakery Company Freaks Out Online After Epic Meltdown on Gordon Ramsey's 'Kitchen Nightmares'* – May 14, 2013 http://www.huffingtonpost.com/2013/05/14/amys-baking-company-kitchen-nightmares_n_3274345.html
3. Marketing, *Is I'm Sorry Enough?* – March 25, 2013 http://www.marketing-interactive.com/is-im-sorry-enough/
4. Andrew Bibby, Profile *Of A Chief Executive: Tan Suee Chieh, NTUC (Singapore)* - 2012 http://www.andrewbibby.com/socialenterprise/ntuc.html
5. Greg Smith, Why I Am Leaving Goldman Sachs – March 14, 2012 http://www.nytimes.com/2012/03/14/opinion/why-i-am-leaving-goldman-sachs.html

6. Nico Nico Douga, *Former Olympus President Michael Woodford Nico Live Appearance* – December 14, 2011 http://live.nicovideo.jp/watch/lv73722602

7. Wikipedia, *Astroturfing* – http://en.wikipedia.org/wiki/Astroturfing

8. The New York Times, *The Best Book Reviews Money Can Buy* – August 25, 2012 http://www.nytimes.com/2012/08/26/business/book-reviewers-for-hire-meet-a-demand-for-online-raves.html

9. Jezebel, *Oh Look A Company Is Paying People To Post Fake Yelp Reviews* – October 2, 2014 http://kitchenette.jezebel.com/oh-look-a-company-is-paying-people-to-post-fake-yelp-r-1641909713

10. American Political Science Review, *How Censorship in China Allows Government Criticism But Silences Collective Criticism* – May 2013 http://gking.harvard.edu/files/censored.pdf

11. The Chartered Institute of Marketing, *Keeping Social Media Ethical* – June 2014

12. Caixin, 删帖生意，一条灰色产业链 – *February 18, 2013*

13. The Guardian, *23 Percent Rise In Defamation Actions As Social Media Claims Rise* – October 20, 2014 http://www.theguardian.com/media/greenslade/2014/oct/20/medialaw-social-media

14. Chris Anderson, *Telephone Interview With The Author* – July 22, 2014

15. Mr Justice Warby, *In Person Interview With The Author* – January 22, 2014

6. Operational and Technological Threats

1. Archanahrdept, *Lemp Experience* – June 11, 2013 http://www.scribd.com/doc/147181239/Lemp-Experience

2. Wikipedia, *Malware* – Retrieved on March 25, 2015 http://en.wikipedia.org/wiki/Malware

3. Wikipedia, *Phishing* – Retrieved on March 25, 2015 http://en.wikipedia.org/wiki/Phishing

4. Kaspersky Lab, *Social Networkers Beware: Facebook Is A Major Phishing Portal* – June 23, 2014 http://blog.kaspersky.com/1-in-5-phishing-attacks-targets-facebook/

5. Greg Mancusi-Ungaro, *Telephone Interview With The Author* – April 3, 2014

6. James Leavesley, *Telephone Interview With The Author* – April 24, 2014
7. Jesper Ingevaldsson, *Robinson's Shoes: Dispute And Subsequent Resolution* – October 9, 2012 http://www.styleforum.net/t/314546/robinsons-shoes-dispute-and-subsequent-resolution
8. SearchEngineLand, *Google Autocomplete: Your Personal Brand's First Impression* – April 18, 2013 http://searchengine-land.com/google-autocomplete-your-personal-brands-first-impression-156002

7. Formulating the Right Response

1. Ed Hoover, *Email Interview With The Author* – December 2014
2. Sam Flemming, In Person Interview With *The Author* – *January 2014*

8. The Furious Customer

1. *FedEx Guy Throwing My Computer Monitor* – December 19, 2011 http://www.youtube.com/watch?v=PKUDTPbDhnA
2. Mail Online, *'This Won't Be His Best Day': FedEx Vows To Track Down Delivery Man Who Tossed Computer Monitor Over Fence* – December 20, 2011 http://www.dailymail.co.uk/news/article-2076432/FedEx-guy-caught-throwing-monitor-fence-YouTube-video.html
3. FedEx, *FedEx Response to Customer Video* – December 21, 2011 http://www.youtube.com/watch?v=4ESU_Pcql38

9. The Rogue Employee

1. Gateflan, *My Mistake, Sir, I'm Sure Jesus Will Pay For My Rent And Groceries* – January 29, 2013 http://www.reddit.com/r/atheism/comments/17i382/my_mistake_sir_im_sure_jesus_will_pay_for_my_rent/
2. Applebee's – February 1, 2013 http://www.facebook.com/applebees/posts/10151390415294334
3. Goldman Sachs, *Our Communication To The People Of Goldman Sachs Regarding The Book By Former Employee Greg Smith* – October 19, 2012

http://www.goldmansachs.com/media-relations/in-the-news/archive/
response-10-19-2012.html

10.   The Committed Activist

1. Shell, *Shell Not Involved In Spoof Video And Fake Advertisements* – July
   19, 2012 http://royaldutchshellplc.com/wp-content/uploads/2012/07/
   spoof-video-fake-adverts-July-2012.pdf
2. Eoin Dubsky, *Greenpeace, The Yes Men And The Inside Story of
   #ShellFail* – June 11, 2012 http://www.greenpeace.org/international/
   en/news/Blogs/makingwaves/greenpeace-the-yes-men-
   and-the-inside-story-o/blog/40893/
3. Daniel Ang, *Calls For Jollibee Singapore Ridiculous And Uncalled For* –
   March 11, 2013 http://danielfooddiary.com/2013/03/11/jollibee-boycott

11.   The Hostile Journalist

1. The New York Times, *Stalled Out On Tesla's Electric Highway* –
   February 8, 2013 http://www.nytimes.com/2013/02/10/automobiles/
   stalled-on-the-ev-highway.html
2. The New York Times, *The Charges Are Flying Over A Test Of Tesla's
   Charging Network* – February 12, 2013 http://wheels.blogs.nytimes.
   com/2013/02/12/the-charges-are-flying-over-a-test-of-teslas-charging-
   network/
3. Elon Musk, *A Most Peculiar Test Drive* – February 13, 2013 http://
   www.teslamotors.com/blog/most-peculiar-test-drive
4. The New York Times, *That Tesla Data: What It Says And What It
   Doesn't* – February 14, 2013 http://wheels.blogs.nytimes.com/2013/
   02/14/that-tesla-data-what-it-says-and-what-it-doesnt/
5. The New York Times, *Conflicting Assertions Over an Electric Car
   Test Drive* – February 14, 2013   http://publiceditor.blogs.nytimes.
   com/2013/02/14/conflicting-assertions-over-an-electric-car-test-drive/
6. The New York Times, *Problems With Precision And Judgment, But
   Not Integrity, In Tesla Test* – February 18, 2013 http://publiceditor.
   blogs.nytimes.com/2013/02/18/problems-with-precision-
   and-judgment-but-not-integrity-in-tesla-test/

7. Bloomberg TV, *Musk: NYT Likely Cost Tesla Hundreds of Orders* – February 25, 2013 http://www.bloomberg.com/news/videos/b/ad03d114-632b-4cc0-bfc3-323b3fdaa74e

8. UC San Diego, *US Media Consumption To Rise To 15.5 Hours A Day – Per Person – by 2015* – November 6, 2013 http://ucsdnews.ucsd.edu/pressrelease/u.s._media_consumption_to_rise_to_15.5_hours_a_day_per_person_by_2015

9. John Cannarella, Joshua A. Spechter, *Epidemiological Modeling Of Online Social Network Dynamics* – January 2014 http://arxiv.org/pdf/1401.4208v1.pdf

10. Facebook, *Debunking Princeton* – January 24, 2014 http://www.facebook.com/notes/mike-develin/debunking-princeton/10151947421191849

11. The New York Times, *The Corporate Daddy* – June 19, 2014 http://www.nytimes.com/2014/06/20/opinion/timothy-egan-walmart-starbucks-and-the-fight-against-inequality.html

12. WalMart, *Fact Check: The New York Times 'The Corporate Daddy'* – June 20, 2014 http://blog.walmart.com/fact-check-the-new-york-times-the-corporate-daddy

12. The Backfiring Campaign

1. Benetton, *Unhate Campaign 2011* – http://unhate.benetton.com/unhate-campaign-2011/

2. ING Direct Canada, *Are You Suffering?* – http://bcove.me/o3lag7dm

3. General Mills, *We've Listened And We're Changing Our Legal Terms Back* – April 19, 2014 http://www.blog.generalmills.com/2014/04/weve-listened-and-were-changing-our-legal-terms-back-to-what-they-were/

13. The Changing Face of Crises

1. Caroline Sapriel, *Effective Crisis Management: Tools And Best Practice For The New Millennium* – February 2003 http://www.csa-crisis.com/info/archives/CS%26A-Journal-of-Comm.pdf

2. BBC, *US Oil Spill: 'Bad Management' Led To BP Disaster* – January 6, 2011 http://www.bbc.co.uk/news/world-us-canada-12124830

3. Freshfields Bruckhaus Deringer, *Containing A Crisis. Dealing With Corporate Disasters In The Digital Age* – November 2013 http://www.freshfields.com/uploadedFiles/SiteWide/News_Room/Insight/Campaigns/Crisis_management/Containing%20a%20crisis.pdf

4. The University of Hong Kong China Media Project, *History of High-Speed Propaganda Tells All* – July 25, 2011 http://cmp.hku.hk/2011/07/25/14036/

5. Ogilvy Public Relations/CIC, *Crisis Management In The Social Era 2013* – July 2014 http://www.slideshare.net/CIC_China/cic-ogilvy-pr-china-released-the-latest-whitepaper-2013-crisis-management-in-the-social-era

14.   Preparing for a Crisis

1. Report of WPC80 Independent Enquiry For Fonterra Board – October 23, 2013 http://wpc80-inde-report.fonterra.com/media/280378/wpc80-inquiry-full-report.pdf

2. Institute for Public Relations, *Crisis Management and Communications* – January 6, 2011 http://www.instituteforpr.org/crisis-management-and-communications/

3. Steven Fink, *Crisis Management, Planning for the Inevitable* (Backinprint.com, 2000)

4. The University of Washington, *Hold That RT. Much Misinformation Tweeted After 2013 Boston Marathon Bombing* – March 17, 2014 http://www.washington.edu/news/2014/03/17/hold-that-rt-much-misinformation-tweeted-after-2013-boston-marathon-bombing/

15.   Responding to a Crisis

1. Najib Razak for the Wall Street Journal, *Malaysia's Lessons From The Vanished Airplane* – May 13, 2014 http://online.wsj.com/news/articles/SB10001424052702303627504579559170123401220

2. Warren Buffett to CNBC, *Goldman Sachs Has 'Lost The PR Battle At This Point'* – May 1, 2010 http://www.cnbc.com/id/36887333/

3. Buffer, *Buffer Security Breach Has Been Resolved – Here Is What You Need To Know* http://open.bufferapp.com/buffer-has-been-hacked-here-is-whats-going-on/
4. Christopher Barger, *The Social Media Strategist* (McGraw Hill, 2012)
5. Kimberly S. Johnson, *Twitter* – June 1, 2009 https://twitter.com/KimberlyReports
6. Scott Peterson, *Telephone Interview With The Author* – August 22, 2014
7. Nuclear Energy Institute, *Tutorials on How Nuclear Plants Work* https://www.youtube.com/playlist?list=PLECE49E00A076C7E9
8. Gallup, *Majority Of Americans Say Nuclear Power Plants In US Are Safe* – April 4, 2011 http://www.gallup.com/poll/146939/majority-americans-say-nuclear-power-plants-safe.aspx

16.   Recovering from a Crisis

1. ABC News, *Lululemon Chairman Chip Wilson's Apology Called Worst Ever* – November 14, 2013 http://www.youtube.com/watch?v=jeFMeBtNRp8
2. JetBlue Corporate Communications, *Our Promise To You* – February 19, 2007 http://www.youtube.com/watch?v=-r_PIg7EAUw
3. Eurostar, *Statement by Richard Brown, Chief Executive* – December 19, 2009 http://www.youtube.com/watch?v=6Jx5EdCEgT4
4. Bronlea Mishler, *Skype Interview With The Author* – August 20, 2014
5. Dell Ideastorm – *Information Retrieved On* April 4, 2015

Twelve Useful Books on Online Reputation

I am frequently asked to recommend good books on online reputation management. A search on Amazon returns over 600 books and e-books on the topic, yet I find myself struggling to recommend a single tome that combines a strategic perspective with practical, how-to guidance. That's not to say that there aren't books on the topic worth reading – there most certainly are and they tackle the subject from all sorts of different angles. Some are general and are aimed at starters, others focus on making the business case to analog senior leaders, many dive deep into the necessarily wide range of tactical activities and disciplines that this area entails.

Whatever your experience and knowledge, here is a selection of books (listed alphabetically) that can help you going forward.

- Jonathan R. Copulsky's *Brand Resilience* (Palgrave Macmillan, 2012) uses the US Army/Marine Corps *Counterinsurgency Manual* (successfully deployed in Iraq, apparently rather less so in Afghanistan) to underpin how companies should plan for and respond to online threats. If the military allegory wears a little thin on occasions, Copulsky's background as a business consultant and marketing expert shines through and provides the book with real authority.

- ie *Brand Vandals* (Bloomsbury, 2013) by public relations agency honchos Steve Earl and Stephen Waddington is packed full of interesting anecdotes and insights into the threats facing brands and companies in the UK (mostly). If light on solutions, *#Brand Vandals* does provide good advice on listening and the kinds of skills that communicators need in order to survive in today's precarious environment.

- Lawyer Andrea Weckerle's *Civility in the Digital Age* (Que/ Pearson Education, 2013) is a useful and highly practical guide to conflict resolution on the web, spelling out the many different types of negative situations in which individuals and organizations can find themselves and setting out the appropriate techniques to resolve them. Comprehensive in itself, *Civility in the Digital Age* also provides a wealth of footnotes for those wanting further information and advice.

- *Navigating Social Media Risks* (Que/Pearson Education, 2012) by Robert McHale is a comprehensive and clear overview of the legal risks associated with social media and digital marketing, covering everything from promotion law, testimonials, and employer monitoring to legal guidelines for developing social media policies and trademark protection. While based on US law, many of the recommended approaches are applicable worldwide.

- As the title says, *Online Reputation Management for Dummies* (John Wiley & Sons, 2012) by Lori Randall Stradtman is a primer for digital immigrants getting to grips with the everyday tasks of building and managing their personal and company's reputations on the internet, from securing domains and establishing online building blocks to creating a digital marketing team and handling bloggers. It also contains pointers on how to deal with negative online reviews and respond to crises.

- *Radical Openness* (TED Conferences, 2013) by Don Tapscott and Anthony D. Williams is not a book about protecting online reputation, rather it details how companies like GSK and Zappos have adopted different approaches to transparency to accelerate speed to market and build trust. Whether or not these approaches have strengthened the reputation of these firms is not substantiated, but there are good reasons to imagine why they might be less likely to be assaulted publicly online.

• Mostly focused on brand-building than reputation protection, Andy Beal's *Repped* (Marketing Pilgrim, 2014) is nevertheless a useful and common-sense guide on how to get your online building blocks in place. It is structured around 30 easy-to-read and follow chapters covering everything from listening and setting up online profiles to creating content, earning reviews, and piquing Google's spiders.

• In *Rethinking Reputation* (Palgrave Macmillan, 2012), Fraser P. Seitel and John Doorley argue that good behavior and transparent communication underpin strong reputations and have underpinned the ongoing success of firms such as Johnson & Johnson and Merck. Of course, these traits also inform organizations looking to rebuild their reputations. The chapter on ExxonMobile's journey from oil spill and environmental whipping boy to engaged global citizen, including its use of social media to build trust and respond to crises, provides much to consider.

• We are all naked on the internet. But some of us, by dint of who we are, how we choose to live our lives, or what we have done in the past are more naked than others. Reputation.com CEO Michael Fertik's *The Reputation Economy* (Crown Business, 2014) makes the case that all of us now need to be extra careful about how we are seen online, which is fast becoming the default source of data when we are being analyzed by potential employers, financial institutions, government agencies, and new acquaintances or lovers.

• The thought of an online crisis makes many people quake, so Ann Marie Van den Hurk has done us a favor by writing *Social Media Crisis Communications* (Que/Pearson Education, 2013). While the author may not be a social media expert she is able to place crises in a broader business and communications context, gives useful tips on how to approach social media operationally, and, best of all, sets out a number of examples of companies responding to negative incidents competently.

- Many people consider reputation management to be a function of public relations first and foremost. Yet public relations people are closely associated with spin doctoring and the manipulation of the media, search engines, and anything else they can twist to their advantage. *Spin Sucks* (Que/Pearson Education, 2014) by PR veteran Gini Dietrich shows the good, the bad, and the ugly of communications today, much of it online, and argues that you can only succeed by being honest, ethical, and educational.

- If you need to understand what it takes to get social media working effectively within a large company, look no further than *The Social Media Strategist* (McGraw Hill, 2012) by Christopher Barger, who spearheaded General Motors' drive into the social web. Excellent for showing how to get a company-wide social media program off the ground and navigate the vortex of internal office politics, it also contains a fascinating blow-by-blow account of how the auto manufacturer used social media to respond to its Chapter 11 bankruptcy in 2009. The latter alone is worth the price.

- Billed as a warts-and-all confessional on modern-day media manipulation and spin-doctoring, Ryan Holiday's *Trust Me, I'm Lying: Confessions of a Media Manipulator* (Portfolio/Penguin, 2012) is also a fascinating and, for those who believe news should be informative and balanced, unedifying glimpse into the inner workings of *Buzzfeed*, *Gawker*, and other blogs re-setting the plate tectonics of the news industry.

Index

Printed and bound by CPI Group (UK) Ltd, Croydon, CR0 4YY